Project Quality Management

Why, What and How

SECOND EDITION

by Kenneth H. Rose, PMP

J.ROSS
PUBLISHING

Copyright © 2014 by Kenneth H. Rose

ISBN-13: 978-1-60427-102-7

Printed and bound in the U.S.A. Printed on acid-free paper.
10 9 8 7 6 5 4 3 2

Library of Congress Cataloging-in-Publication Data

Rose, Kenneth, 1947-
  Project quality management : why, what and how / by Kenneth H. Rose, PMP.
Second edition.
        pages cm.
  Includes bibliographical references and index.
  ISBN 978-1-60427-102-7 (pbk. : alk. paper)
  1. Project management. 2. Quality control. I. Title.
  HD69.P75R664 2014
  658.4'013—dc23
                                                2014011089

Direct all inquiries to J. Ross Publishing, Inc., 300 S. Pine Island Rd., Suite 305, Plantation, FL 33324.

Phone: (954) 727-9333
Fax: (561) 892-0700
Web: www.jrosspub.com

Dedication

Thank you, Nancy, for your love and support over the years.

This book is dedicated to our son, Geoffrey—a good person and a good engineer.

Table of Contents

Preface

This book is a product of frustration. Quality is clearly one of the key components of project success. Everyone talks about quality. Everyone demands and promises quality in project implementation. But in the end, it seems to be much mentioned and little employed. The reason why is not difficult to identify or understand. Many quality tools—indeed many quality books, lectures, and training sessions—seem to be oriented toward the manufacturing domain. A discussion of methods and tools may start off generally enough, but as soon as examples enter the discussion, they leap right back to some kind of manufacturing environment. That may be fine for shop supervisors, but it provides little information of relevance to project managers who work with intellectual processes more than the action details of production.

So where does a project manager go for guidance on how to integrate quality into project implementation? Many years of searching have yielded few results. There just do not seem to be any good sources that deal directly with both quality of the *project* and quality of the *product*. Project managers are busy people. They want answers, not a lot of Socratic questions or a lot of theory followed by good wishes for subsequent application.

This book delivers what has been missing. It provides a background of quality concepts and their evolution over time, but is focused on the limited information that is necessary for project managers to understand the context of quality. It summarizes concepts in a model of contemporary quality that provides a unifying, big-picture view. It provides a simple framework of specific action steps to manage project quality. It explains key quality tools relevant to the framework and presents them in a logical order of application.

Finally, the book takes readers through a practical exercise in a management environment that will allow them to experience an application—to *do* something—not just read about one.

The first edition enjoyed considerable success. It won the coveted 2006 PMI® David I. Cleland Project Management Literature Award from Project Management Institute. It was the object of much interest among professionals and received a surprisingly high and consistent level of interest among academics. It is used in courses and certificate programs at universities in the U.S. and in Australia, Brazil, Canada, and Venezuela.

Because of the strong academic utilization, this second edition has been expanded to include features tailored to classroom use. Each chapter now offers a series of review topics and questions that will challenge reader/student knowledge about the content. Each chapter also offers a series of practical exercises that require readers/students to apply what they learned to real-world situations associated with their own experience or in their own context. Example cases related to key quality management processes illuminate the processes in a real sense and show readers/students how they apply in practice.

This second edition has been updated throughout. References and citations have been brought up to current texts, including the *PMBOK® Guide—Fifth Edition*. Content has been expanded and clarified where necessary, including an enhanced discussion of quality assurance as a unique process, separate from quality planning and quality control. A new final chapter, "Why *Not* Quality?" explains why quality can be an elusive goal, even in organizations with requisite knowledge and intent. Comprehensive monographs that address the related issues of project training, project leadership, and organizational change management appear as new appendices. The appendix on project leadership may be of special interest and offer special value as it explores the matter in a unique way, unlike much of the current literature.

This book will not make you an expert on quality. It will not enable you to lecture long and eloquently about the history and theory of quality. It *will* give you an immediate hands-on capability to improve project implementation and customer satisfaction by making quality an integral part of your projects and the products of your projects. That is probably what really matters anyway.

About the Author

 **Kenneth H. Rose** completed a twenty-three-year military career in high-technology development and project management as a member of the Army Acquisition Corps. His hands-on experience ranges from the first steps of initiating concepts, identifying user requirements, and evaluating technology alternatives to the culminating processes of project implementation and delivery. Subsequently, as senior research scientist with Pacific Northwest National Laboratory, he helped large government organizations to develop and apply quality improvement programs, innovative performance measurement procedures, and strategic plans. As a project manager for a not-for-profit affiliate of Virginia Tech, he led projects and performed technical work related to environmental activities, project management training and implementation, and organization development and leadership. He is currently Director, Peninsula Center for Project Management, Hampton, Virginia, USA, providing project management consulting and training services.

An accomplished author, Mr. Rose began writing articles for professional and technical journals in 1985. Known for a penetrating and engaging style, he has been published in widely read periodicals such as *Quality Progress*, *PM Network*, *National Defense*, and *Military Review*. His first book, *An Introduction to Artificial Intelligence: A Self-Study Text*, was used at the U.S. Army Computer Science School in the 1980s to provide a grounding for students in this emerging technology. Ken's contributions to technical literature were recognized by the Project Management Institute by being selected as the winner of the 2006 David I. Cleland Project Management Literature Award for *Project Quality Management: Why, What and How* in its first edition. The PMI® David I. Cleland Project Management Literature Award recognizes the author(s) of a single publication that most significantly advanced project management knowledge, concepts, and practice in the year it was published.

Current writing efforts are focused on analyzing new project management literature. His book reviews of new project management texts appear in every issue of *Project Management Journal* (online version).

Mr. Rose holds a Master of Arts degree in management from Ball State University and a Bachelor of Fine Arts degree in music theory and composition from the University of Wisconsin-Milwaukee. He is a member of the Project Management Institute, a certified Project Management Professional (PMP®), and serves as book review editor of *Project Management Journal*, the academic-research publication of PMI. He is a former senior member of the American Society for Quality and a former ASQ Certified Quality Manager. He is a life member of the National Defense Industrial Association and past chairman of the robotics division.

Web
Added
Value™

This book has free material available for download from the
Web Added Value™ resource center at *www.jrosspub.com*

At J. Ross Publishing we are committed to providing today's professional with practical, hands-on tools that enhance the learning experience and give readers an opportunity to apply what they have learned. That is why we offer free ancillary materials available for download on this book and all participating Web Added Value™ publications. These online resources may include interactive versions of material that appears in the book or supplemental templates, worksheets, models, plans, case studies, proposals, spreadsheets and assessment tools, among other things. Whenever you see the WAV™ symbol in any of our publications, it means bonus materials accompany the book and are available from the Web Added Value Download Resource Center at www.jrosspub.com.

Downloads *Project Quality Management, 2nd Edition*, include numerous tools for planning project quality, collecting and understanding data, comprehending and analyzing processes, and problem solving, as well as instruction materials for use in college and professional courses on the topic.

Section I

Quality Foundations

1

Understanding Quality in the Project Management Domain

What is quality? Customers know it when they see it. Suppliers promise that their goods and services embody it. Both views are often missing a clear, up-front definition of what quality is, and this leads to confusion and frustration when trying to determine just how to deliver it.

Project managers probably feel this most acutely. A customer may demand quality and an organization may promise to deliver quality, but a project manager is the one who has to do it. Failure can have devastating immediate and long-term consequences for both the project manager and the project organization.

Given its importance to project outcomes, quality ought to be a problem long ago solved. It is not. Projects continue to be plagued by imprecise quality goals and arcane quality methods most suited for a shop floor, all of this condemning the project to less-than-satisfactory results or worse.

There is a better way. From a product manufacturing or service delivery point of view, quality is, to a great degree, a problem solved. Quality tools and techniques have been developed and refined over the past 100 years to the level that they are now a matter of science, not art. Applying these proven ways to project management should be a simple matter of transference, but that is the problem. Projects come in many stripes and colors. A project undertaken by a national professional association to create a new technical manual has little relation to the codified quality tools of manufacturing, except in the final steps of producing the book itself, and that task is usually contracted to a source outside the project team.

Definition of Quality

The key to project quality lies in making a more effective, meaningful transfer of proven quality methods to a general project management domain. The first step is to answer the question "What is quality?"

> **Exercise 1**—Consider the question "What is quality?" for a few moments. Take time to do this seriously. Put this book down, get out a blank sheet of paper, and think about the question in depth. What does quality mean to you? What might it mean to others? How do you describe quality to others? How do you know quality when you see it? What are quality's component elements? Make a few notes, then continue reading.

The results of this brief exercise probably vary among individuals. Some central themes may be common to all.

- ◆ **Products**—In some way, quality is associated with products. This may be the most obvious linkage. We define quality by our view of the features or attributes of some particular product: an automobile, an article of clothing, an electronic device, and so on. This view can lead us with confidence to the destructive "I'll know it when I see it" definition of quality.
- ◆ **Defects**—The idea of defects in a product is closely related to the view of products themselves. The perception of product quality may arise from favorable features, such as an automobile that always starts on the first attempt, or is comfortable on long trips, or exhibits efficient fuel consumption. Defects are a bit different. We expect quality products to be free of defects. When we purchase a car, the upholstery should not be ripped or soiled, all the indicator lights on the dashboard should function properly, and there should be no cracked mirrors or light covers.

◆ **Processes**—Now things get a little more obscure. If we manufacture a product, we probably care very much about processes. To the users of our product, the matter of processes tends to be rather transparent. Users focus more on the product and how it performs than on how it was produced. This issue is also very important to project managers. Whether they are delivering a product that results from manufacturing or purely intellectual activity, the processes that produce that product have great effect on the outcome. *What* you do may keep a smile on your customer's face, but *how* you do it will keep you on schedule and on budget—and that may make the customer's smile even brighter and longer lasting.

◆ **Customers**—People who sell what they make may be very product focused in their view of quality. They seek to make products that are superior to those of competitors and always strive to be the best: "This is the best DVD player on the market today." This view of quality may have short-term utility, but can be limiting, even lethal, for the organization in the long term. Consider the boasts "This is the best carburetor on the market today" or "This is the best buggy whip on the market today." Both statements may be true, but if nobody is buying carburetors or buggy whips, are they relevant? People who make what other people want to buy have a different view of quality and it is rooted in what customers want. To these people, quality is defined by customers, their needs, and their expectations.

◆ **Systems**—A system is a group of things that work together. At a higher level of analysis, quality may be viewed as arising from things that work together. Products, defects, processes, and customers are all part of a system that generates quality, as are suppliers, policies, organizations, and perhaps some other things unique to a specific situation.

Traditional Definitions

Several definitions of quality already exist. In the now obsolete 3rd edition of his ground-breaking *Quality Control Handbook*, quality pioneer Joseph M. Juran defined quality as "fitness for use." In this view, customers defined the use for the products (goods or services) that they purchased. It was up to the organization that produced the products to understand the needs of its customers and to design products that are fit for use. In *Juran's Quality Handbook*, 6th edition, a revised definition appears. Quality is now "fitness for purpose."[1] This new view is intended to be broader in scope and more universal in applicability, especially for service organizations that have risen to a larger role in the world economy since the appearance of the original definition.

Juran recognized the shortcomings of such a brief definition. He emphasized that the definition of quality includes two components that are critical to its management. Quality includes *"features that meet customer needs."* These features should, among other things, increase customer satisfaction, prevail over the competition, and enhance product sales. Because more or better features add to design, it is reasonable to say that higher quality costs more. Quality also includes *"freedom from failures."* These failures may be errors during production that require rework (doing something over again) or failures in the field after purchase that may result in warranty claims, customer dissatisfaction, or dire consequences to the user. Because an absence of failures means an absence of associated costs, it is reasonable to say that higher quality costs less.

Juran also made a distinction between "Big Q" and "Little Q." The concept of Big Q is a more recent development, arising in the 1980s, and is more systems-wide in its approach. It takes a broader view of quality that encompasses the goals of the enterprise and all its products. It is usually embraced by quality managers and senior managers within the organization. Little Q is more limited in scope, often focused on individual products or customers. This view is usually embraced by those in technical or staff functions.

The Project Management Institute defines quality as "the degree to which a set of inherent characteristics fulfill requirements."[2] This definition is taken directly from *ISO 9000:2005*, published by the International Organization for Standardization.[3] The ISO 9000-series standards are a group of international consensus standards that address quality management. *ISO 9000:2005* is a brief introductory standard that covers fundamentals and vocabulary. This definition is most complete because it is so general. The set of inherent characteristics may be of a product, processes, or system. The requirements may be those of customers or stakeholders, an important group that is ignored at great peril to the success of the project.

One important aspect of quality does not come out in any of these definitions. Quality is "counterentropic"; it is not the natural order of things. Entropy, from the Second Law of Thermodynamics, says that things naturally move from a state of organization to a state of disorganization. Drop a handful of mixed coins on the floor and the result is not an array lined up in rows by type. The result is a bunch of coins spread randomly across the floor. So it is with quality. However it is defined, quality is not a naturally occurring event. It is a result of hard, deliberate work that begins with planning, includes consideration of contributing elements, applies disciplined processes and tools, and never, ever ends. Achieving quality in project implementation is not a matter of luck or coincidence; it is a matter of management.

Quality and the Triple Constraint

The project "triple constraint" includes time, cost, and scope. All three elements are of equal importance to project success and to the project manager. Project managers typically try to balance the three when meeting project objectives, but they may make trade-offs among the three during project implementation in order to meet objectives and satisfy customers. Quality is a fourth among equals. It may be most closely associated with scope because scope is based on customer requirements and quality is closely associated with customer requirements. This linkage addresses quality of the *product* of the project. There is another important quality consideration: quality of the *project* itself. Quality processes, attuned to the scope specifications, will ensure a quality product. Quality processes that maintain cost and schedule constraints will ensure a quality project. Some recent project management literature suggests that quality is part of a quadruple constraint consisting of time, cost, scope, and quality. This approach is wrong-headed for one simple reason: Project managers routinely make trade-offs among the triple constraint to meet project objectives. A project manager should never, never, ever trade off quality during project implementation.

Cost of Quality

Much misunderstanding exists about quality in spite of the various definitions in circulation. Quality is many things to many people, but quality is also *not* some things that have been assumed over time.

- ◆ **An expensive process**—One of the first questions asked when a quality improvement effort is proposed is "How much will this cost?" This is always a valid question, but an uninformed view can produce an invalid answer. Conventional wisdom, perhaps better called "conventional ignorance" in this case, has it that better quality costs more. In times of cost control and cost cutting, the answer to quality improvement can be an unwise "We can't afford that." Philip B. Crosby, another quality pioneer, addressed this in a book entitled *Quality Is Free*. Briefly, his point was that quality does not cost, it pays. When you improve the quality of a process, you reduce the defects that result from that process. While the new process may be more expensive—it may be less expensive, too—the resulting reduction of defects is something that pays back over and over and over. So if the payback is more than the cost, as it often is, quality is essentially free.

◆ **An expensive product**—This may be the greatest misunderstanding of all because of the tendency to view quality in terms of products. An automobile with leather seats and little mechanical wipers on the headlights costs more than one without these features. A fine "writing instrument" costs more than a plastic ballpoint pen. But price does not confer quality. Review the definitions of quality. None of them mentions price. Quality arises from an ability to satisfy customer needs. If a customer's goal is to spend a lot of money, then an expensive product may be viewed as top quality. Customers generally seek the lowest price for a product that meets their functional needs, not the highest. Considering accuracy and maintenance, an inexpensive digital watch from a drugstore provides better quality than a more expensive mechanical watch from a jewelry store. A customer may want the jewelry item, but only because it serves a purpose other than timekeeping, not because it is a better quality watch.

◆ **Time consuming**—"We don't have time" is the response that condemns an organization to poor quality. Urgency prevails and shipping dates or field requirements rule. The reality is that we always have time; we just choose not to use it wisely. The old adage "There's never enough time to do it right, but always enough time to do it over" is not just a clever collection of words; it is the truth. Poor quality in production leads to rework. Delivery of poor quality products leads to replacement, warranty charges, lost customers, and loss of reputation. In the long run, quality saves time and much, much more.

Crosby's statement that quality is free is good theory. In practice, quality does have costs, even if those costs are subsequently outweighed by benefits. The sources of cost of quality are three: failure, prevention, and appraisal.

Failure

Failure costs may result from either internal or external failure. The major costs associated with internal failures, those that occur before a product has been delivered to a customer, are scrap and rework. At the end of some process, a product may not conform to prescribed specifications. The degree of nonconformance may be so severe that the product cannot be fixed and must be discarded. Any costs associated with production to this point are lost. This is scrap. In some cases, the degree of nonconformance may not be so severe. A reasonable amount of additional effort may bring the product into conformance, so the product is re-entered into the process and any additional work adds to the overall cost of production. This is rework. The costs of scrap and rework are more than the sum of lost product and additional work. Costs associated with disposal, storage, transportation, and inventory control must be included to determine total costs.

External failures, those that occur after a product has been delivered to a customer, may generate costs for repairs in accordance with product warranty obligations. They may also generate product recalls, which can be far more expensive. Consider the potential cost of fixing a defective part during assembly versus recalling 1.2 million automobiles to replace the defective part. Recall costs are orders of magnitude higher than repeat costs.

An external failure may also generate liability costs that are far more expensive. A coffeemaker that is improperly marked or includes defective temperature controls may produce coffee that scalds unsuspecting customers. Or worse, an automobile may be so poorly designed that when struck from the rear in an accidental collision, the fuel tank ruptures and ignites the fuel, which causes immolation of any passengers in the car. The cost in human suffering and loss of life cannot be calculated, but courts will do the best they can. Resulting awards in compensatory and punitive damages can be astronomic.

External failure costs include those associated with complaints and complaint handling. Organizations must pay specially skilled staff members to receive and respond to complaints. These employees must be empowered to offer satisfaction of various kinds, all of which have a cost. Loss of customers is a cost of nonconformance that has been characterized as unknown and unknowable.[4] Suppose a woman buys an expensive silk blouse at a high-end boutique. She wears it to a special event where a careless guest spills something on it. She has it dry-cleaned, but notices on its return that one of the side seams has opened up. She takes it back to the boutique where her money is promptly returned because the shop stands by its products. Is the woman a satisfied customer? Sure, she got her money back, but what about all the inconvenience and disappointment? Will she ever shop there again? There is no way to tell because no device has yet been invented that will count the number of customers who do not come back through the front door. And what about her friends who will never shop there after hearing about her bad experience? Again, no device exists that will count the number of customers who do not come through the front door initially. There is a bit of wisdom in retail sales regarding the buying habits of dissatisfied customers: "The goods come back, but the customers don't."[5]

Beyond costs, the effects of failure are significant and many. The effects begin with dissatisfied customers. Satisfied customers can serve as unpaid sales representatives. Without coaching or any expectation of reward, they will sing the praises of an organization and its products to all who will listen. Dissatisfied customers do just the opposite, and research shows they do so to a greater degree than satisfied customers. With a corps of complainers working against them, organizations may experience a loss of customers, which leads to loss of business, loss of revenue, loss of jobs, and eventual failure of the organization. Failure cost is not a trivial matter to be accepted or analyzed away in a spreadsheet.

Prevention

Prevention costs are fundamentally different from failure costs. These costs are related to things that an organization does rather than to outcomes of a process. Prevention costs begin with planning. One of the greatest errors a project manager can make is to leap into performance without sufficient planning. Planning may be limited for many reasons, none of them very good. Urgency may be a reason, but if the need for the product is so urgent, the product should be right when delivered. Management's desire to cut costs may be a reason, but would management be willing to fund the effort required to do the work over and make it right if it is not when delivered? Planning generates early costs to be sure, but good planning prevents later costs that arise from changes to an inadequate plan. The cost of changes goes up as the project progresses. Changes made during implementation are far more expensive than changes made during planning. Good planning prevents later costs.

Prevention costs include both quality planning and audits, and process planning and control. Quality planning establishes the quality management system for the project. Quality audits ensure that the system works as intended. Generally, an audit is a comparison of performance to plan. A quality audit compares the performance of the organization or project quality system to the quality plan. Audits have an associated cost, which may recur with every audit. The results of quality audits show that the quality system is working or show that it is not working and must be improved. The subsequent result of either outcome is an effective quality system that reduces defects and costs associated with those defects.

Process planning establishes the steps to be taken to produce the product of the project. Process control ensures that the process performs as expected. A well-trained work force may produce defective products if the established processes are not capable of producing a high degree of conforming product. Processes tend to be rather static, but other things in the system (materials, management, working conditions, tools, requirements) change around them. Processes must be monitored and analyzed to ensure that they are current with the need of the organization and not something that is done because it seemed like a good idea at the time of implementation. Process planning will cause an organization to incur a cost for the plan and additional costs for control activities and process improvements, but these costs will pay back in reduced defects over time.

Product reviews constitute another prevention cost. Customer coordination and requirements definition, internal design reviews, and reliability engineering all generate early costs that contribute to quality of the final product.

Suppliers are a critical component of quality. Costs related to evaluating suppliers and their quality management systems are prevention costs.

A well-trained worker and a well-trained work force are more likely to produce products that conform to specifications. Less-trained workers may not possess the ability to perform according to specifications. They may not recognize nonconformance with specifications, and they may not even know what the specifications are. When a worker produces an item that is so defective that it must be discarded (scrap), the organization incurs a cost for every item discarded ... again, and again, and again. When the organization trains the worker to perform better, it incurs a one-time cost for the training and obtains cost savings from the reduced number of defects produced by the worker as a result of the training. The training pays the organization back ... again, and again, and again.

Appraisal

Appraisal costs begin with inspection of incoming supplies. The computer science phrase "garbage in, garbage out" applies equally here. The quality of a product is significantly affected by the quality of materials that go into its production. Supplier evaluations may have determined that a particular supplier will provide what is needed for a project, but inspection of actual deliveries is both prudent and essential. Some years ago, an army engineering center was fabricating special devices for clearing land mines in desert terrain. A supplier initially delivered inferior quality steel that did not meet specifications and would have endangered the lives of those depending on the devices.

In-process product inspection is a form of appraisal that ensures production is following the plan. Noted deficiencies may be corrected before the end of the process when scrap or additional-cost rework are the inevitable results. Final product inspection determines conformance of the result of the complete process.

Performance of well-known products may be predicted with some certainty. Buy a ream of copy paper and it is likely to work as expected in the office copy machine. New products do not enjoy the same degree of certainty in eventual performance. Testing will verify performance before the product is finished and delivered. Testing has a cost, but it is another appraisal cost that pays back over time in reduced rework of products that do not perform precisely as specified.

The effects of prevention and appraisal are simple and straightforward: better products, better processes, more capable workers, and more satisfied customers. The big difference between prevention/appraisal costs and failure costs is that failure costs are responses that occur repeatedly over time; prevention/appraisal costs are investments that provide cost benefits repeatedly over time.

Benefits of Quality

The benefits of quality in project performance are many. First, a quality project and product will yield customer satisfaction. If you meet or exceed requirements and expectations, customers will not only accept the results without challenge or ill feeling, but may come back to you for additional work when the need arises. They may well become that oh-so-important unpaid sales representative and generate additional work from new customers through referrals. A satisfied customer may perceive greater value than originally anticipated, which goes beyond customer satisfaction to customer delight.

Reduced costs are another benefit. Quality processes can reduce waste, improve efficiency, and improve supplies, all things that mean the project may cost less than planned. As costs go down, profits may go up (depending on the pricing arrangement in the contract on which the project is based) or reduced costs may mean more sales to an existing customer within existing profit margins.

Finally, better products, better project performance, and lower costs translate directly into increased competitiveness in an ever-more-global marketplace. This is the essence of a quality chain reaction described by W. Edwards Deming: improve quality, reduce costs, improve productivity, capture the market, stay in business, provide more jobs.[6]

Summary

- ◆ Quality involves products, defects, processes, customers, and systems.
- ◆ Quality is the ability of a set of inherent characteristics of a product, system, or process to fulfill requirements of customers and other interested parties.
- ◆ Quality is a fourth among equals in relation to the project triple constraint of time, cost, and scope.
- ◆ Quality is not an expensive process, an expensive product, or time consuming.
- ◆ The cost of quality may be viewed in terms of internal and external failure to conform to specifications (recurring costs) or prevention of nonconformance and appraisal (investments, recurring benefits).

◆ The effects of failure to conform to specifications may include dissatisfied customers, loss of customers, loss of business, loss of revenue, and failure of the organization.

◆ The effects of prevention and appraisal may include better products, better processes, more capable workers, and more satisfied customers.

◆ Quality benefits include customer satisfaction, reduced costs, increased profits, and increased competitiveness.

Points to Ponder

1. Describe several views of quality in the context of your own knowledge or experience. Include at least three of the following: products, defects, processes, customers, systems, or others.

2. Select a product (goods or services) about which you have some personal knowledge. Explain how Juran's two components of features and freedom from failures relate to the quality of that product.

3. Discuss the cost of quality considering failure, prevention, and appraisal costs. Give examples from your own knowledge or experience.

4. Explore specifically the costs of internal and external failures. Which one can be more expensive? Give examples, imagined or from your own experience.

5. From your own experience—school, work, social organizations—describe the benefits of quality in real-world situations. Give examples.

Exercise

a. Prepare a matrix that explores Juran's concept of "fitness for purpose." In the first column, list at least six examples of products: two hard goods, two services, two elements of information. In the second column, describe the fitness for purpose for each example. In the third column, describe aspects of quality that may come into play in establishing fitness for purpose. In the fourth column, describe actions that may be taken to influence the quality aspects. If so inclined, add a last column as a clearinghouse to address related matters that may have arisen in your work.

b. Prepare a presentation of the results of your matrix for class or for a collaborative work group. Lead a discussion among participants.

References

1. Juran, J.M. and De Feo, J.A., Eds., *Juran's Quality Handbook*, 6th ed., Mc-Graw-Hill, New York, 2010, pp. 5.
2. *A Guide to the Project Management Body of Knowledge—Fifth Edition*, Project Management Institute, Newtown Square, PA, 2013, p. 228.
3. *ISO 9000:2005, Quality management systems—Fundamentals and vocabulary*, International Organization for Standardization, Geneva, 2005, p. 7.
4. Deming, W.E., *Out of the Crisis*, The MIT Press, Cambridge, MA, 2000, p. 121.
5. Ibid., p. 175.
6. Ibid., p. 3.

2

Evolution of Quality and Its Contemporary Application to Projects

---

The concept of quality did not leap into existence fully formed. It evolved over time. It developed in progressive steps that responded to the needs and limitations of the times.

Progressive History

The historical development of quality concepts may be traced by examining major themes that held sway during various times. In some cases, these themes followed practice. In other cases, they made new practice possible and advanced the overall concept of quality.

The Dark Ages

The march of quality began during the age of craft production, the 1700s and before. During this period, individual craftsmen produced items for use by others. The craftsmen were totally responsible for the product from start to finish. Consider Paul Revere, an American silversmith in Boston in the late 1700s. He was personally responsible for all aspects of what he produced. He designed the items, obtained supplies, developed production techniques, probably made many of his tools, sold the items to customers, and

17

handled any complaints. He also received any suggestions or requests for custom-made items. He made the items one at a time, and each one was just a little different (perhaps in ways indistinguishable to the casual observer) from any other similar item.

Craftsmen had complete responsibility for, and total control of, the output of their work. They probably acquired their skills by watching and working with someone who was very good at the specific skill. Paul Revere probably served as an apprentice to a master silversmith before he established his own business. Schools and training courses with highly codified, standard procedures did not exist. Apprentices learned and adopted the ways of the master, perhaps later developing new methods that might result in better products, shorter or more efficient procedures, and increased competitiveness. Craftsmen worked in the home or a shop closely associated with the home. Today, visitors to Colonial Williamsburg in Virginia or similar historical sites may view such craftsmen at work, including silversmiths, gunsmiths, and coopers (barrel makers).

The need for more items, produced faster, put a fatal strain on craftsmen. Work began to move to central locations where many workers combined their efforts toward a common goal. Factories arose and the industrial revolution changed production in ways that emphasized quantity and commonality. The production of a teapot, which Paul Revere made himself from start to finish, was broken down into tasks. Individual workers were responsible for only a part of the final product. Often, the workers did not even have a view of what the final product was; they were only responsible for their particular piece.

An element of craft production still existed in factories. Workers were generally highly skilled because work was done by hand, but now the focus was on individual parts, not the whole. It was important that parts be very similar to each other so that they might be assembled into a final product without significant modification. Inspection became an important aspect of production to ensure that parts met some established design standard. Workers were the critical element in production; they were held responsible for the outcome. The quality philosophy in play at the time might best be stated as "If you want to make the boat go faster, whip the oarsmen harder."

Scientific Management

Frederick Winslow Taylor saw things a bit differently. In his view, if you want to make the boat go faster, you should examine and analyze those things that make the boat go and determine the best way to do it. In other words, it is not *what* you do, but *how* you do it that counts. In 1911, he published *The Principles of Scientific Management*, which described his approach. Taylor suggested that in getting things done, there is "one best method," and it is management's responsibility to determine that method and the worker's responsibility to follow established procedures. Taylor changed the focus from the worker to the process and, most significantly, separated planning and execution. Planning was a responsibility of management; execution was a responsibility of workers.

Taylor's approach broke the mold of worker-focused quality, but failed to recognize two key aspects of quality. The first is motivation. Taylor assumed that workers were principally motivated by money. He described a "high-priced man" as a worker who will perform according to management's prescribed procedures for money. The other is his assumption that once an optimal procedure is defined, the results will be the same for every worker. Taylor's scientific management involves one way of doing something, one standard worker, no variation in performance, and no communication between workers and management.

Understanding Variation

The next leap forward occurred when Walter Shewhart expanded the quality focus to include variation. In 1918, Shewhart was a newly hired physicist working at Western Electric's Bell Laboratories. At that time, radio was a relatively new invention being applied to military use. Shewhart was assigned a project to develop a radio headset for the military. The headsets had to fit comfortably, so "head breadth" (the physical distance between the ears) was one of the factors to be considered. When analyzing head breadth data provided by the military, Shewhart noticed an orderly distribution. Some people had wide heads, some had narrow heads, and a lot fell in between. The data seemed to follow a normal distribution pattern.

Shewhart wondered if manufacturing processes employed at Western Electric might exhibit the same kind of variation. He began to study the issue and this became a primary interest for the rest of his career. Shewhart's studies revealed that almost all types of *repeatable* processes exhibit variation. The key is *repeatable* processes. If you do something the same way over and over, the results will not be exactly the same. They will be similar, but will vary to some degree in predictable ways. Shewhart found this phenomenon in both manufacturing and administrative activities.

Over time, Shewhart developed methods for analyzing and understanding this variation. His work became a foundation for doing something about the variation, not just observing it. In 1931, he published *Economic Control of Quality in Manufactured Products*, which outlined the principles of statistical process control (SPC), a disciplined approach for improving quality by reducing variation in the process. In 1939, Shewhart published another book, *Statistical Method from the Viewpoint of Quality Control*, which introduced the plan-do-check-act cycle as a means of implementing quality improvements (see Chapter 6 for further discussion).

Inspection Reigns

Variation meant potential waste. If a product varied too far from a target, it had to be redone or discarded. During World War II, the demand for manufactured products of many kinds increased dramatically. Military customers had urgent requirements that would not tolerate a lot of scrap and rework. At the same time, shortages of materials required efficient utilization of what was available. Shewhart's SPC techniques were put to good use by industrial suppliers of military goods. W. Edwards Deming, who had worked with Shewhart at Western Electric, helped the War Department apply Shewhart's methods. Conformance to specifications became the central focus of quality, and inspection (comparing final results to targets) became the primary method of achieving conformance.

It would be nice to believe that wartime requirements moved quality forward, but they did not. Urgent requirements demanded shorter production times and that, in turn, reduced quality. The tendency arose to ship products that were *close enough* to target because the military forces in the field needed them *right now*.

After World War II, the United States had very little industrial competition because of wartime damage to facilities in other countries. Producers became complacent. SPC withered as an unnecessary expense. Postwar managers did not take time to understand the benefits of SPC. Quality matters became a function of organizational quality departments. Quality became a numbers game involving the number of charts rather than the meaning of the data, or the number of people trained rather than the improvement that resulted from the training. Inspection departments flourished as the quality focus drifted back to conforming within an acceptable level of error.

Japanese Quality

Not everyone was complacent, however. In Japan, members of the Japanese Union of Scientists and Engineers considered quality a key component in rebuilding the country's industrial base in ways that would enhance international competitiveness. They invited experts from other countries to come to Japan and share their methods. W. Edwards Deming was one of the first. In 1950, he presented a series of lectures to leaders of Japanese industry. The Japanese participants were much taken by both Dr. Deming and his ideas. They listened carefully and took steps to put quality concepts into practice, particularly SPC.

Other American quality pioneers participated. Joseph Juran visited and provided a more strategic view that expanded quality methods to all functions within an organization, not just the shop floor. His definition of quality as "fit for customer use" changed the focus from conformance to specification to meeting customer expectations. Armand Feigenbaum's "total quality control" approach integrated the various departments in an organization so that quality became a way of life—all elements of an organization working together toward the same goals.

For their own part, Japanese engineers and managers added internal customers to the quality equation, those elements of a process that receive input from others and act on it in some way before providing it to the next element in the process. They added the concept of quality circles—small groups of workers and managers who work together to solve a problem—a far cry from Taylor's "do what management says" approach. And perhaps of most significance, they added the concept of *kaizen*—continual, incremental improvement. Quality was no longer a destination based on conformance to requirements; it became a journey that never ends.

As a result, Japan became a global economic superpower within twenty years. The label "Made in Japan" attached to simple products like a small bamboo umbrella served with an exotic beverage was once a source of mild derision. Because of Japanese quality achievements, it became a label of respect, denoting items that did what customers expected them to do, worked the first time, and did not fail during use.

Customers and Systems

In the contemporary view, customer requirements define quality, not products or processes. In other words, it is not *what* you do or *how* you do it, but *who uses it* that counts. Quality is in the perception of the customer. Using the classic example from quality literature again: You can make the best buggy whip that was ever made, using the finest materials and applying efficient processes that have almost no defects or waste, but if nobody needs a buggy whip, it just does not matter.

Many things work together to yield products that meet customer requirements. Viewing these things independently can lead to competition among the elements that interferes with the desired quality outcomes. Viewing these things as a system allows integrated consideration and optimization of the whole for the customer's benefit. Elements of a quality system include external customers, internal customers, suppliers, materials, processes, policies, tools, skills, capabilities, and even society as a whole.

Quality Then and Now

Contemporary quality concepts might be best understood by way of comparison to what existed previously, a comparison of quality then and quality now. In recent times past, quality comprised three elements: inspection, statistics, and rework. At the end of some production process, a result was inspected to determine its degree of conformance to specifications. The degree of conformance was usually stated in terms of a range of values to account for process variation. Statistical techniques were applied to determine the acceptable level of performance. Organizations might establish an "acceptable quality level" of 99.995 percent for a particular process; that is, no more than 5 defects per 100,000 results. Items that were judged to be defective were reinserted into the process for additional work at additional cost to bring them into conformance or discarded if the defects were so severe that the item could not be fixed economically. Higher levels of quality usually meant higher costs because more defective items fell into the unacceptable category and had to be either reworked or discarded.

Contemporary quality comprises a significantly different set of elements: customer focus, variation, and continuous improvement. Quality begins with an understanding of customer requirements as the base. Customer requirements establish the performance goals for the organization. Variation is an

Table 2.1. **Quality Then and Now**

Quality Then	*Quality Now*
Inspection: Inspect something at the end of production to determine if it meets specifications	Customer focus: Customer requirements are the base
Statistics: Establish statistical goals for conformance	Variation: Understand it, control it
Rework: Fix (or discard) nonconforming product	Continuous improvement: Products and processes improve forever

omnipresent aspect of every process. It cannot be wished away or analyzed away through statistics, which ultimately accept the variation and change the process expectations around it. Instead, variation is understood and controlled using statistical methods that determine its predictability. Continuous improvement begins with the state of the current process as statistically defined and identifies opportunities for modifications to the process that will reduce the degree of variation, which in turn reduces defects and increases consistency and predictability of performance (see Table 2.1).

The Wheel of Quality

The concepts of contemporary quality are codified in a single graphic image as seen in Figure 2.1. This graphic displays the three elements of customer focus, variation, and continuous improvement, showing the relationships and interactions among them. It also adds the essential elements of training and leadership.

Customer Focus

Projects have more than one customer. The tendency is to view the person or organization that pays the bills as the only customer or the only customer of any importance. A more savvy view recognizes the existence of a number of customers that generally fall into three categories.

The first is a group of external customers—those outside the organization or the project team. The client is the most obvious external customer, being the one who usually pays the bills and verifies project completion. Suppliers are also external customers. This can seem a bit counterintuitive because, by

Figure 2.1. The Wheel of Quality. (Copyright © 2003 Kenneth H. Rose)

definition, the project team is a customer of the supplier. However, suppliers must understand the requirements of the project team in order to deliver supporting goods and services that meet the needs of not only the team but also the customer of the team. So, the team must view suppliers as customers of well-defined and timely requirements. In addition, a client may obtain products and services for another party, an end user. An obvious and often-used example is dog food. The end user of the product is the dog that either eats or rejects the food. The client is the dog owner who either buys or rejects the food initially. Marketing and sales efforts are directed toward the client, not the end user, but the end user must be considered throughout the project to develop, produce, and sell the product.

Internal customers constitute another category. A project, unless it is extremely simple, is usually completed by a number of collaborating elements within an organization. Each element performs a piece of the work and passes its piece on to another element that will perform another piece and pass it along to another and another until the final product is delivered to the client. These collaborating elements have a supplier-customer relationship to each other. Each element produces something as a supplier that is passed along to another element that receives it as a customer. Projects may involve complex networks of internal customers that are critical to project success. Simply stated, an internal customer is the next step in the process chain.

Hidden customers can be the most difficult to identify and the most troublesome for project managers. Hidden customers are stakeholders—people or organizations that do not participate directly in the project, but have an interest in or concern about the project to the degree that they may want to influence the outcome. Some may be apparent; initiate a project to deploy a statewide wireless network and a government regulator (such as the Federal Communications Commission) will pop up as a hidden customer. Some are not apparent; these tend to be the dangerous ones as they can appear out of nowhere and put a project off track. Wireless network implementation may be going according to plan until a local group files a stop-work lawsuit because people do not want any communication towers in their backyard.

Customers are important for many reasons. An unknown source suggests that people who do not think customers are important should try to do business without them for a while. Customers buy our products. They buy our products repeatedly. They tell their friends to buy our products. They define needs for new products. They indicate interest in, or a lack of interest in, or even opposition to, potential products. And perhaps most important of all, they complain and give us valuable information and insight for improving our products.

All of this suggests a customer role that falls into four parts:

1. **Provide needs and requirements**—Customers are important because they are the source of requirements that are the foundation for the project.
2. **Define performance**—Beyond requirements, customers describe "how well" a product should perform. They provide measurable targets.
3. **Evaluate products**—Customers will accept or reject products based on the degree to which the products meet their expectations.
4. **Provide feedback**—Customers will comment, complain, recommend, or purchase a product again.

Variation

Repeatable processes do not produce precisely repeatable results. Variation is a characteristic of any production process, but it is not a great mystery. Variation can and must be understood and controlled in order to influence results. The unique aspects of projects can lead managers and team members to believe that everything they do is unique and that variation is not an issue. Project managers may have to spend a little time to determine what tasks within a project, or between projects, involve repeatable work. Doing so is an early step toward improved quality.

This is an important matter because variation can produce defects. After identifying sources of potential variation, project managers must seek to understand the variation, why it occurs, and what its effects are. Then they must control the variation so the process involved performs consistently, producing predictable results. Improvement occurs when project managers or members of the project team analyze the process and take action to reduce the variation to some degree. If the process is routinely producing results that lie outside established specifications, it must be fixed immediately. Subsequent actions should reduce variation further, which results in a higher number of conforming products or products that conform more closely to the target value. As an example, the "Six Sigma" approach to quality management establishes a goal of process variation so narrow that product specifications encompass six standard deviations above and below the mean when performance results are plotted on a curve. The practical result, adjusted to allow a slight shift in the mean over time, is no more than 3.4 defects per million. (Six Sigma is discussed further in Chapter 3.)

Project managers and other levels of management are primarily responsible for quality. This obligation is based on a principle credited by various sources to both Joseph Juran and W. Edwards Deming. It is the "85/15 rule," which states that 85 percent of workers' performance is determined by the system they work within and 15 percent is determined by their own individual effort. Management, not individual workers, is responsible for the system. Therefore, when seeking improvement in a process, project managers should first analyze and fix the system, not blame the workers. In the same way, project managers should be careful about rewarding individual workers for system performance over which they had no influence. Rewarding people for the wrong things can be just as harmful to organizational cohesion and morale as blaming people for the wrong things.

Continuous Improvement

Continuous improvement can be a thorny issue for project managers. Projects based on an external contract have explicit specifications—obligations in the contract. A practical approach may be to "meet specifications" because that is what is required and that is all that is paid for. In fact, "quality" is defined by some as "conformance to requirements," suggesting that meeting specifications achieves quality. Superficially, meeting specifications is the goal. The Project Management Institute makes much of this, stating that this is all a project manager should do; anything beyond is "gold plating." This makes good sense. Gold plating (adding expensive features to a product that go beyond the original scope, but do not add anything of value to the customer) should be avoided, but in a wider view, meeting specifications may be doing *just enough* work to escape punishment. The result may be a satisfied customer, albeit a *minimally* satisfied customer. Meeting specifications also constrains project performance to the limits of the specification or the customer's understanding of technology or what is possible. It does not give the customer a better solution if one is possible. It does not enhance organizational competence unless specifications have been set challengingly high, something contract managers are reluctant to do. Meeting specifications can mean safe, routine performance that does not enhance organizational competitiveness. Specifications provide a conundrum that is simply stated:

> If you don't meet the specifications, you are in breach.
>
> If you want to complete the current contract, meet the contract specifications.
>
> If you want to win the next contract, meet or exceed the customer's expectations.

Continuous improvement involves at least three specific actions. Communication is essential. The project team must have effective communication within itself and with customers, suppliers, and stakeholders. Communication is the means of identifying problems and opportunities, resolving problems, and exploiting opportunities.

Corrective action is also essential. Fixing problems is necessary, but not sufficient. Project managers and team members must also identify the causes of any problems and eliminate them or reduce them to the greatest extent possible. It is good to fix a problem; it is better to prevent it from occurring again.

Identifying and acting on opportunities completes the three. The plan-do-check-act cycle provides a disciplined approach for continuous improvement based on either identified problems or opportunities.

The results of continuous improvement may be incremental small steps or dramatic great leaps forward. Both types of results provide common benefits to the performing organization that enable it to:

◆ **Meet dynamic needs and requirements**—Customer needs are always changing. Give them what they ask for and they will ask for more.

◆ **Stay competitive**—Competitors are always improving. The global marketplace is not in a steady state; it is a race, and you cannot win a race by standing still.

◆ **Reduce costs, increase profits**—The global marketplace includes competitors with very low costs, particularly in labor. Reducing costs can increase competitiveness, which will increase sales and overall profit.

◆ **Develop new technologies, processes, and products**—Technology is always changing. Improving processes to take advantage of new technology or simply to employ a better way can reduce costs, provide a better product, or both.

Training and Leadership

Training is the foundation of quality. Action should be based on well-grounded theory, not trial and error, how things have been done before, or the desire or dictum of an individual. Members of the project team, including the project manager, must be trained in all necessary skills. Members new to the team during implementation must be trained also, not simply placed on the job and admonished to learn from others. Appendix 2 provides additional information on project training.

Leadership is the unifying force of quality. The goals of leadership are to improve performance and quality, increase output, and bring pride of workmanship to people.[1] Leadership is necessary to eliminate the *causes* of defects, not just the defects alone. To be effective, leaders must know the job. They must be technically competent in the work at hand and capable in purely leadership skills in order to earn the respect and commitment of team members and to represent the project team well with customers, stakeholders, and upper management within the organization. Appendix 3 provides additional information on project leadership.

The Wheel of Quality Model

The graphic image of The Wheel of Quality discloses how all these elements interact. Customer focus, variation, and continuous improvement are the central issues in contemporary quality. Each is related to the others and shares a common boundary. Each is expressed through a more specific aspect of project work—respectively, requirements, processes, and controls.

These aspects are not discrete, but exist as a spectrum between two extremes. Requirements may range from general needs to explicit specifications. Processes may be viewed from those focused on outputs or products, which interface with the explicit specifications of requirements, to general techniques. Controls may focus on means of production, which interface with the techniques of processes, to ends of production, which interface with the general needs of requirements, completing the linkage of all three aspects.

These aspects are further linked by higher level considerations in the organization that bridge the aspects two at a time. What we do bridges requirements and processes, how we do it bridges processes and controls, and why we do it bridges controls and requirements.

As the foundation of quality, training is the hub of the wheel. Without training, project team members will be unable to employ the three elements effectively. Leadership holds it all together. Leadership encircles all elements, aspects, and considerations in a continuous outer loop that binds them in a unified whole.

Quality and Responsibility

Given all this, a simple question remains: Who is responsible for quality? In times past, the quality department was responsible, but no more. Quality departments have been significantly reduced and functions have been transferred to the performing level or eliminated altogether. Nowadays, everyone is responsible for quality. Organizational management is responsible for the quality system. Project managers are ultimately responsible for project and product quality. Project teams are responsible for the quality aspects of their part of the project, and individual team members are responsible for quality in everything they do to contribute to project completion. No one has the luxury of off-loading quality responsibility to someone else or some other function. Everyone associated with a project is responsible in some way, with the project manager bearing the burden or obligation of ensuring quality in everything the project does.

Summary

♦ Contemporary quality arose through an evolution from craftsmen totally responsible for quality, to factories that distributed tasks and quality responsibility, to scientific management that focused on processes rather than individual workers. It further developed through an understanding of process variation and an understanding of the role of customers and systems.

♦ The traditional quality approach involved inspection, statistics, and rework. The contemporary approach involves customer focus, variation, and continuous improvement.

♦ Training and leadership are essential to contemporary quality.

♦ The Wheel of Quality graphically displays the elements of contemporary quality and the interrelationships among them.

♦ Everyone is responsible for quality. The project manager is ultimately responsible for project and product quality.

Points to Ponder

1. Discuss quality in the era of craft production. Who was responsible for quality? How were customer requirements determined? How did design and production influence quality? How was consistent quality maintained? Other aspects?

2. Describe Taylor's concept of scientific management and how it influenced quality. Who was responsible for what? How was Taylor's concept a step forward? What was not addressed?

3. Explain Juran's view of variation and how it influenced quality. Give some examples of variation in both manufacturing and administrative contexts. How can variation *within* a project come into play? How can variation *between* projects come into play?

4. What is the role and importance of inspection in quality performance? How can inspection hinder quality? Describe some good ways of using inspection to achieve quality results.
5. How did Japanese scientists and engineers expand the view of quality? What were the benefits?
6. Discuss the role of customers in quality. Why are they important? What do they influence?
7. What are the basic elements of a quality system? What is the role of each element? How do they interact?
8. Describe quality "then" and "now." How may one approach be more effective than the other?

Exercise

a. Prepare an annotated Wheel of Quality for a product (goods or services) that you know something about. Draw the Wheel on a large sheet of flip-chart paper so you have room to fill in the various sections with examples. List customers, processes, and controls. Show how the listed elements form a spectrum and how the endpoints of the spectrum link together. Show leadership and training contributions.
b. Present your results in class or to a collaborative work group.

Reference

1. Deming, W.E., *Out of the Crisis*, The MIT Press, Cambridge, MA, 2000, p. 248.

3

Pioneers and Paradigms

Contemporary quality is what it is today because of the combined contributions of pioneers who made breakthrough advances by developing, describing, and deploying new techniques. Over time, new methods were integrated into existing frameworks or coalesced into entirely new frameworks that provided comprehensive, systematic approaches to quality.

Pioneers

The few included here are principal pioneers, well known for achievement and approach. Many others contributed, some probably unnoticed or unrecognized.

Walter Shewhart

Shewhart was mentioned previously in Chapter 2. His work at Bell Laboratories was the foundation for statistical techniques that brought consideration of variation into the mainstream of quality. Accordingly, Shewhart has been called "the father of statistical quality control." He was acquainted with W. Edwards Deming and Joseph Juran and mentored them both in their early careers.

In his 1931 book, *Economic Control of Quality of Manufactured Product*, Shewhart identified two types of variation: chance cause, which was inherent in the system and could not be individually identified, and assignable cause, which was an exception in the system and could be individually identified and removed. He developed techniques for collecting and analyzing data that would show the difference between these two sources of variation and allow improvement by eliminating assignable cause variation. He later developed and described the plan-do-check-act cycle, a disciplined approach to quality improvement that will be discussed in detail in Chapter 6.

W. Edwards Deming

Deming is perhaps the best-known quality pioneer. His approach to quality was statistically based, but focused on responsibilities of management. While others focused on details, he maintained a broad, almost philosophical, view that considered quality in overall economic terms. His "chain reaction," mentioned in Chapter 1, is a good example of his wide-ranging approach. Early in his career, he worked at Western Electric's Hawthorne plant, where he came into contact with Walter Shewhart. In the 1940s, he assisted the U.S. Census Bureau in applying statistical sampling techniques. During World War II, he worked with U.S. defense industries to improve the quality of military items through statistical processes.

After World War II, Deming went to Japan under government sponsorship to assist with a population census. While there, he was invited by the Japanese Union of Scientists and Engineers to present a series of lectures on statistical quality control techniques. He found a copy of Shewhart's 1931 book in a library at General MacArthur's headquarters in Tokyo and used it as a foundation for the lectures. The Japanese participants were much taken with Dr. Deming and his ideas. They listened carefully and applied what they learned energetically and relentlessly. Japan's national quality award, the Deming Prize, is named in his honor. Dr. Deming was also much taken by the Japanese pursuit of quality. He commented later in life that no population in his worldwide experience equaled the dedication of Japan's.

Deming never established a short, single theory of quality. Instead, he developed a list of fourteen goals or admonitions that he called "fourteen points for management." He strongly believed that these points were the foundation for a transformation of American industry. He viewed quality as an obligation of management. He did not view with great kindness what he saw as the traditional American approach of blaming quality problems on workers. During his lectures in Japan, he bluntly told participants to import American quality techniques, but not to import American management techniques. The fourteen points, in a somewhat abbreviated form, are shown in Table 3.1.

Table 3.1.　Deming's Fourteen Points for Management.

1. Create constancy of purpose for improvement of product and service.
2. Adopt the new philosophy.
3. Cease dependence on mass inspection.
4. End the practice of awarding business on the basis of price tag alone.
5. Improve constantly and forever the system of production and service.
6. Institute training.
7. Adopt and institute leadership.
8. Drive out fear.
9. Break down barriers between staff areas.
10. Eliminate slogans, exhortations, and targets for the work force.
11. Eliminate numerical quotas for the work force; eliminate numerical goals for people in management.
12. Remove barriers that rob people of pride of workmanship.
13. Encourage education and self-improvement for everyone.
14. Take action to accomplish the transformation.

From Deming, W.E., *Out of the Crisis*, The MIT Press, Cambridge, MA, 2000, pp. 24–86.

The fourteen points must be taken as a whole. Piecemeal or partial adoption will not suffice, and no individual point is more important than another. Later in life, Deming expressed some regret that he had numbered the points because people assumed that the numbers indicated priority of performance, something Deming had not intended at all.

Dr. Deming also identified practices that could prevent completion of the transformation, calling them the seven "deadly diseases." Some are closely linked with quality practice within an organization. Others relate to external, even national, issues of finance, health care, and law. The seven deadly diseases are shown in Table 3.2.

Toward the end of his career, Deming formulated what he called a system of profound knowledge that comprised the four elements necessary for transformation to the new style of management:[1]

1. Appreciation for a system
2. Knowledge about variation
3. Theory of knowledge
4. Psychology

Table 3.2.   Deming's Deadly Diseases.

1. The crippling disease: lack of constancy of purpose

2. Emphasis on short-term profits

3. Evaluation of performance, merit rating, or annual review

4. Mobility of management

5. Running a company on visible figures alone (counting the money)

6. Excessive medical costs

7. Excessive costs of liability

From Deming, W.E., *Out of the Crisis*, The MIT Press, Cambridge, MA, 2000, pp. 97–121.

These interrelated elements are discussed at length in Dr. Deming's book *The New Economics for Industry, Government, and Education.*

Joseph M. Juran

Juran also presented quality lectures in Japan. His approach to quality focused on strategic and planning issues. He believed that poor quality results from inadequate or ineffective planning, so he proposed the Juran Trilogy, a three-step approach to quality that includes quality planning, quality control, and quality improvement.[2] His view that quality has two aspects—product features and freedom from failures—was mentioned in Chapter 1. *Jurans's Quality Handbook,* 6th edition, edited by Juran and Joseph A. De Feo, is the most comprehensive quality book on the market today.

According to Juran, quality improvement depends on two different activities: control and breakthrough. Control ensures that processes are performing consistently, free of assignable cause variation. Breakthrough occurs after a process has been studied and some major improvement has been designed and implemented. He suggests that these activities are not separate and sequential; they can and should occur simultaneously.

Juran is also known for Pareto analysis, a quality technique based on a principle from economics. This will be discussed in detail later, along with the associated quality tool, the Pareto chart. Briefly, Pareto analysis recognizes that all possible contributors to defects in a product are not equally responsible for results. A small number of contributors are usually responsible for most defects. The goal is to identify that small number (the "vital few") and eliminate them.

Philip B. Crosby

Crosby viewed quality as conformance to requirements. Further, he saw no reason for nonconformance. Acceptable levels of quality established on a statistical basis were simply recipes for failure. Quality was a result of prevention of defects, not inspection and subsequent correction of defects. He believed that the goal of any process should be *zero defects,* and this term soon became a widespread mantra in government and industry.

A major tenet of his approach was that quality is free; that the cost of quality is eventually outweighed by the benefits and, therefore, is not a cost at all. Crosby focused on behavioral and motivational aspects of work rather than statistical aspects of processes. Of all the pioneers, he was perhaps the most successful at selling his ideas through consultation and training.

Not everyone agreed with Crosby's approach, however. Juran thought quality was not at all free. He believed that quality improvement efforts would experience diminishing returns; that initial efforts would yield cost favorable results, but later efforts would yield less value and constitute a true expense. Deming viewed zero defects as insufficient. Customer satisfaction (the thing that keeps a company in business) depends on many things other than the number of defects.

Kaoru Ishikawa

Ishikawa's enormous influence on quality is often unrecognized simply because his contributions have become so ingrained that they seem a natural part of things. He brought customers into the quality equation, redirecting focus to them rather than the methods of production. He emphasized training and education of workers as a foundation of quality. He created quality circles, increasing the role of workers in solving problems and identifying opportunities for improvement. Taking this further, he emphasized total involvement of employees in improving quality and coined the phrase "company-wide quality control." Throughout his life, he provided a model of selfless dedication to quality that inspired others around the world.

Under his leadership, the Japanese Union of Scientists and Engineers adopted training as a primary mission. One of Ishikawa's greatest achievements was the codification of basic quality tools that fit well within the quality frameworks presented by Deming and Juran. His *Guide to Quality Control* is an international classic that concisely defines what have become known as the "seven basic tools" of quality. Written for workers, not statisticians, the book is credited with democratizing statistics and making these techniques accessible to those who really need to use them.

Genichi Taguchi

Taguchi is best known for his innovative approach to quality known as "the Taguchi method." It is a follow-on to Shewhart's work in statistics and Deming's work in quality improvement. Many consider the method to be equal in stature to the contributions of Deming and Ishikawa.

The Taguchi method considers quality not as conformance to specifications, but as a target within a range. The target value provides ideal quality. Deviations from the target are expressed in a quality loss function. Instead of an acceptable level of variation within a specified range, all variation is viewed as some degree of cost to the customer, the supplier, or society in general. Consider the local pizza parlor. Both its profit and reputation are dependent on the amount of cheese on the pizzas it sells. So it establishes a target value, say eight ounces for an extra-large, and prices the item accordingly. Deviations above target will increase the cost of the product to the owner and deviations below target will generate customer dissatisfaction, which is also considered a cost. Traditionally, the owner would establish an acceptable range of variation, say seven to nine ounces, and manage to that range. Taguchi said that every degree of variation has a cost to either the owner or the customer. Those costs are captured and disclosed in the quality loss function. The Taguchi method also employs a three-step process of robust design that uses Design of Experiments to determine which elements of a process have the greatest effect on the outcome and statistical methods to produce results that are high quality and defect free.

Paradigms

Evolving quality concepts are captured in a number of formalized frameworks. Project managers should be aware of several of the principal paradigms. Not all may be applicable to a particular project. Each may provide some benefit, depending on the goals of the project team.

Six Sigma

In the mid-1980s, the U.S. electronics firm Motorola set out to make a great leap in defect reduction—not just a small step, but an orders-of-magnitude reduction. It called the approach "Six Sigma." The name comes from the Greek letter *sigma* (σ), which is used in statistics and quality as a symbol for standard deviation. From basic statistics, the area under a standard normal curve (a "bell-shaped" curve) encompassed by three standard deviations above and below the mean is 99.73 percent of the total curve. By extension, a process that produces results that show plus or minus three standard deviations from the mean within specifications is producing 99.73 percent acceptable product, or only 27 defects per 10,000. That may seem like good performance, but it is not. Twenty-seven defects in every 10,000 items produced can be very expensive. Motorola did not establish a three-sigma target; it established a target of six sigma. In other words, the goal was to reduce variation so far that the results provided plus or minus six standard deviations from the mean within specification.

Technically, six standard deviations above and below the mean encompass 99.9999998 percent of the standard normal curve, or two defects per billion. Motorola modified the percentages to allow for a 1.5-sigma shift in the mean over time, understanding that processes may drift a bit. The result is a six sigma goal that, in Motorola parlance, is 99.99966 percent, or 3.4 defects per million. Results were not trivial. Over ten years, Motorola achieved $414 billion in savings, a five-times increase in sales, and a 20 percent annual increase in profits. The concept was subsequently applied at General Electric and Allied Signal with beneficial results. The Six Sigma approach is not for everyone. It is intended for, and works best in, high-volume production environments.

Six Sigma has, in some ways, taken on a life of its own. Cynics may see it as "the next big thing" that will fade as soon as a new buzzword comes along. In a practical view, however, it seems to have some staying power. Currently, the approach has two aspects: management and methods. Application begins with a management initiative that recognizes the goal as breakthrough, great-leap-forward improvement, not incremental improvement. It involves a systematic and focused approach that is highly disciplined. Success depends on selecting the right projects, those that support the strategic goals of the organization, not the most convenient, the most troubled, or the boss's favorite. Selecting and training the right people to lead the effort and carry through is critical. A Six Sigma effort is not a short-term opportunity for corporate job hoppers. Implementation requires effective project management and comprehensive, no-nonsense reviews of progress. Any gains must be sustained and institutionalized. All of these elements combine to produce the right results—process improvements that improve the bottom line and global competitiveness.

Six Sigma methods and tools arise from common quality practice. The Six Sigma approach begins with process thinking that considers inputs, outputs, and both controlled and uncontrolled variables. Variation is a foundation of the approach, with the goal being to reduce variation around the mean and to move the mean closer to the target value if necessary. Six Sigma depends on data-based decisions, so data, facts, and figures play a key role. Standard quality tools and statistical tools are employed throughout implementation. Because statistics are so important, user-friendly statistical software has been developed that is specifically oriented toward Six Sigma application. The "vital few" variables are the focus of attention, not the whole range of possible variables.

These tools are all integrated into a standard methodology designated by the acronym "DMAIC," for define, measure, analyze, improve, and control:

- **Define** customers and requirements
- **Measure** things critical to quality
- **Analyze** baseline, opportunities, objectives, and root causes
- **Improve** the process
- **Control** the process

ISO 9000

The International Organization for Standardization (ISO) is a global body headquartered in Geneva, Switzerland, that develops consensus standards for worldwide use. The organization's short title "ISO" is not a fractured acronym, but rather an adaptation of the Greek word *isos*, which translates to English as "equal." The American National Standards Institute (ANSI) is the U.S. member of ISO. The American Society for Quality (ASQ) is a member of ANSI and is responsible for quality management standards. It publishes standards in the ANSI/ISO/ASQ-Q9000 series that are the U.S. equivalent of standards published by ISO.

The ISO 9000-series of standards addresses quality management systems. The series includes three standards:

1. *ISO 9000, Quality management systems—Fundamentals and vocabulary*

2. *ISO 9001, Quality management systems—Requirements*
3. *ISO 9004, Quality management systems—Guidelines for performance improvements*

ISO 9001 is a *specification* standard. If an organization wishes to become certified or registered—the terms mean the same thing, only the conventions of use differ—it would have to conform to the requirements in *ISO 9001*. Organizations can self-declare conformance or can hire a third-party registrar. Third-party certifications are generally viewed as more objective. *ISO 9004* is a *guidance* standard. It provides additional, useful information about quality management. Nothing in it is required for certification. Generally, *ISO 9004* contains elements on which international consensus could not be reached and, therefore, could not be included in *ISO 9001*. Neither *ISO 9001* nor *ISO 9004* are performance standards. They do not address quality itself, only the management processes necessary to achieve quality. Various editions of the ISO standards include dates in the reference number. The *ISO 9001* standard may be listed as *ISO 9001:2008* to indicate the 2008 edition.

The initial motivation for applying *ISO 9001* may be commercial. Many international customers favor suppliers that are certified. Once organizations see the benefits of a quality management system, they may continue regardless of specific commercial pressures. *ISO 9001* is a brief document. It contains many prescriptive paragraphs that indicate what an organization "shall" do. Conformance requires extensive documentation, including:

◆ **Quality policy**—A statement from top management.
◆ **Quality manual**—A document that addresses each clause in *ISO 9001*. Specific procedures may be part of the manual or referenced in the manual.
◆ **Quality objectives**—Goals assigned to organizational elements.
◆ **Quality procedures**—Step-by-step actions for each *ISO 9001* requirement or any process that affects quality.
◆ **Forms, records, documentation**—Proof of performance.

ISO 9001 implementation provides many benefits. It forces analysis of quality management activities. In the absence of a disciplined form of management, quality can be one of those things assumed to be done. It documents all aspects of the quality management system—again, no assumptions or promises, only facts. It focuses on prevention, not inspection. The *ISO 9001* approach is prevention based, an approach proven to be more effective in the long run than identifying and fixing accepted defects as they occur. Finally, it is a framework for quality improvement. Continual improvement, not satisfaction with the status quo, is an essential part of the *ISO 9001* approach.

Baldrige National Quality Program

The Baldrige National Quality Program is a public-private partnership administered by the National Institute of Standards and Technology (NIST), an agency of the U.S. Department of Commerce. Its goal is to improve performance of U.S. organizations. It recognizes outstanding quality performance with the annual Malcolm Baldrige National Quality Award. Between 1988 and 2013, 1601 applicants won a total of 102 awards. Currently, up to eighteen awards may be made among seven categories: business/nonprofit (manufacturing, service, small business, nonprofit, government), education, and health care. The awards are announced at an annual awards ceremony in Washington, D.C. and presented by the President of the United States.

The award is based on evaluation of criteria in seven categories. A total of 1000 points is distributed across the criteria. Separate criteria are published for the business/nonprofit, education, and health care areas. Award criteria for the 2013-2014 business/nonprofit category are shown in Table 3.3.

Organizations considering application should obtain the criteria documents pertaining to their area (education, small business, and so on). The application process requires submission of an eligibility certification package to determine eligibility of the organization for the award. The application requires answers to about one hundred questions spread across seventeen items in the seven categories (2013-2014 business/nonprofit criteria). Scoring is a two-step process involving an individual evaluation by an examiner, then a consensus examination by a small group of examiners. Organizations that score highly are selected for a site visit during which examiners confirm the data contained in the application. Selection of winners follows, with subsequent announcement and presentation of the award.

The award itself, though prestigious, is not the only way an organization can benefit from the Baldrige National Quality Program. Any organization may complete a self-assessment using the award criteria and gain insight into its quality performance. Application documents contain clear and specific descriptions of criteria and scoring procedures. Applying these criteria can

Table 3.3. Malcolm Baldrige National Quality Award Criteria.

Categories	Points
Leadership	120
Strategic Planning	85
Customer Focus	85
Measurement, Analysis, and Knowledge Management	90
Workforce Focus	85
Operations Focus	85
Results	450
Total Points	1000

be a stand-alone effort for internal benefit or the first step in a complete application process. One bit of cautionary advice regarding self-assessment: Beware of overstating the results. Organizations will not benefit from an unrealistically optimistic evaluation approach. It must be a warts-and-all view, regardless of the discomfort such a view may cause to some within the organization. If an organization tends to punish the bearers of bad news, it probably is not on very solid quality ground to begin with.

Closing Thoughts

Quality is hard work and it is situation dependent. There is no cookbook, no magic formula, no plug-and-play. There is no instant pudding.[3]

Summary

- ◆ Walter Shewhart developed statistical techniques for analyzing, understanding, and controlling process variation.
- ◆ W. Edwards Deming assisted the U.S. Census Bureau and U.S. defense industries in applying statistical techniques. He presented quality lectures in Japan that helped initiate that country's quality efforts. His view was that quality is a responsibility of management. His fourteen points for management provide guidance on quality.
- ◆ Joseph Juran's view of quality focused on strategic and planning issues. He developed Pareto analysis to identify the "vital few" variables that account for the majority of defects in a system.

- Kaoru Ishikawa brought a new focus on customers, training, and total employee involvement to quality. He codified the seven basic tools of quality.
- Genichi Taguchi developed the Taguchi method that includes a quality loss function and robust design to achieve quality.
- Six Sigma is a framework for quality that seeks to reduce variation to the point where a process produces only 3.4 defects per million. A standard approach includes the five steps of define, measure, analyze, improve, and control.
- ISO 9000 is a series of international consensus standards for quality management systems. *ISO 9001* is a specification standard that prescribes what an organization must do to achieve ISO certification.
- The Malcolm Baldrige National Quality Award is a U.S. national award that recognizes quality performance. Organizations may use the award criteria to perform a self-assessment and gain benefit without actually applying for the award.

Points to Ponder

1. Discuss the principal contributions of Walter Shewart to quality, including the two types of variation he described.
2. Describe the overall contribution of Deming's "Fourteen Points" to quality. Pick three that might apply to your personal experience and discuss in detail. How does each point lead to improvement?
3. Explain the difference between Juran's concepts of control and breakthrough.
4. Summarize Crosby's concept of "quality is free." From your personal knowledge and experience, what activities contribute to quality? Is quality really free?
5. What were the major contributions to quality by Ishikawa and Taguchi?
6. What are the foundation and goals of the Six Sigma approach to quality? Is this a universal approach that may be applied to all activities in all domains?
7. Describe the ISO 9000 approach to quality. What is the basic goal? What are the key elements?
8. Explain the purpose of the Malcolm Baldrige National Quality Award. How might it be used internally for an improvement effort?

Exercise

a. Obtain a copy of the award criteria for the Malcolm Baldrige National Quality Award. Pick a category (business/nonprofit, education, health care) in which you have interest, experience, or a personal connection. Using the criteria, design a project for self-assessment. If possible, implement the project and collect results.

b. Present a description of your project or the results of its implementation in class or to a collaborative work group.

Suggestion: In an academic setting, conduct this exercise as a class project or as a project by a group or multiple groups of students. Obtain a copy of the criteria for the education category. It is available online from the Baldrige Award web site for a small fee. A self-assessment tool is also available free of charge. In 2013, the Pewaukee School District in Wisconsin won an award. Winners are required to share their experience with others. Contact information and summary information is available on the Baldrige Award web site.

References

1. Deming, W.E., *The New Economics for Industry, Government, and Education,* 2nd ed., The MIT Press, Cambridge, MA, 2000, p. xv.
2. Juran, J.M. and De Feo, J.A., Eds., *Juran's Quality Handbook,* 6th ed., Mc-Graw-Hill, New York, 2010, p. 78.
3. Deming, W.E., *Out of the Crisis*, The MIT Press, Cambridge, MA, 2000, p. 126.

Section II

Quality Management

4

Project Quality Planning

So, you have the contract. Now what? Or you have just received the directive from management to initiate an internal project. Now what? What exactly should you do next to ensure that quality is built into the project? The answer lies in the component parts of quality management.

Quality Management

Many approaches to quality management exist. Every consultant with a laptop and flip chart probably has a proprietary approach that is advertised as the one best method. Taking a broader view, the *PMBOK® Guide* describes three elements of quality management: quality planning, quality assurance, and quality control. The Juran Trilogy describes three slightly different elements: quality planning, quality control, and quality improvement. In Juran's view, quality assurance is similar to quality control but performed by those not directly involved in producing the product. Juran also adds the essential element of quality improvement, which the *PMBOK® Guide* does not include as a distinct process. Our approach combines the best of these two views to include quality planning, quality assurance, quality control, and quality improvement.

The *PMBOK® Guide* states that project quality management "… includes the processes and activities of the performing organization that determine quality policies, objectives, and responsibilities so that the project will satisfy the needs for which it was undertaken."[1] This description is sufficiently general to cover the needs of the project in terms of time, cost, and scope and the needs of the product of the project or customers of the project in terms of the defined requirements. Project quality management is linked to overall organizational quality management in terms of processes and costs.

Quality Planning

The *PMBOK® Guide* defines its Plan Quality Management process as "The process of identifying quality requirements and/or standards for the project and its deliverables and documenting how the project will demonstrate compliance with quality requirements."[2] This activity is the foundation for quality being *planned* in, not *inspected* in. Project managers need not, and must not, depend on inspection and correction to achieve project quality. Instead, they should use conformance and prevention to achieve quality. Project managers should, through planning, design in and build in quality.

Quality Management Plan

The basic document for project quality is the quality management plan. It is one of the several subordinate management plans within the project plan. When faced with an unfamiliar task (as quality management often seems to be), project managers may look for an existing template to apply as a starting point. Few such templates exist. Quality management plans are more described than demonstrated in project management literature. That may be beneficial to project managers. Applying a template may not allow consideration of the subtle aspects of a project that are inherently unique. It may be best for project teams to craft an individual quality management plan that fits the needs of the project, not just the format of a published template. A general framework for quality management plans includes four elements:

1. **Quality policy**—This "… establishes the basic principles that should govern the organization as it implements its system for quality management."[3] One of the best examples of a clear, concise quality policy (though probably not so named at the time) is "We shall build good ships here; at a profit if we can, at a loss if we must, but always good ships" (Collis P. Huntington, Newport News Shipbuilding and Dry Dock Company, 1893). The project team may simply apply the existing organizational quality policy, but only if it is a good fit. Needs of

the project may demand a quality policy that is more specific than a generally stated organizational quality policy.

2. **Who is in charge?**—This question is one of three that lie at the heart of quality management. The answer is neither trivial nor simple; it is not just the name of the project manager. A complete answer—one essential to project success—addresses project and organizational infrastructure and describes participants, reporting chains, and responsibilities. There are few more certain paths to project failure than an ambiguous collection of participants in which everyone is in charge, but no one is responsible.

3. **Where are we going?**—Managing quality effectively depends on specific performance targets. Goals provide broad descriptions of what the project is expected to achieve. Requirements provide more detailed descriptions. Operational definitions, which describe what something is and how it is measured, provide the means for understanding goals and requirements that may be vague or ambiguous.

4. **How are we going to get there?**—The answer to this question should address processes, resources, and standards. Processes define the things the project team will do to meet requirements and achieve project goals. The quality management plan may include a lengthy list of processes covering many different aspects of project work. Resources include more things than money. This part of the plan should describe the people available, participating organizational elements, tools to be used, and, of course, the budget that provides funding for all quality activities. Standards to be applied to project work are an important element of this part of the plan. Remember that, by definition, quality planning is about identifying quality standards.

Identifying Customers

Customers were discussed previously in Chapter 2. Customers are the base. To reiterate, customers may be classified as external (the paying client, suppliers, and end users), internal (elements in the supplier-process-customer chain), and hidden (those not directly involved, but concerned about the project's outcome). All of this is rather straightforward. Internal customers may be the most difficult to identify. A simple graphic may help (see Figure 4.1).

Identifying customers is not a matter of intuition or guesswork. Identification involves four explicit steps:

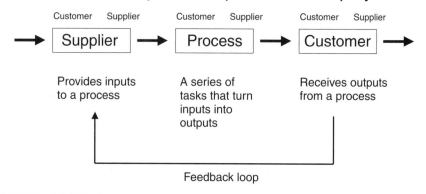

Figure 4.1.   Internal customers.

1. **Analyze the contract**—As a first step, analyzing the contract will identify an important external customer, the paying client. This analysis may also identify an end user. If the end user is not clear from the contract information, the project team may have to coordinate directly with the paying customer to determine if the end user is someone other than the paying customer. Contract analysis may also reveal suppliers. If key suppliers are not specifically identified as subcontractors, the project team may have to coordinate among its own technical elements or with the organization's procurement office to determine what suppliers will be part of project implementation.
2. **Analyze the project team and organization**—This is the step that identifies internal customers. Analysis should disclose how work will proceed—what project team or organizational elements will participate and how they will be linked together in the supplier-process-customer chain.
3. **Analyze product use**—This step starts with the end user and goes a bit further to identify more specifically who will use the product and how they will use it. Remember, quality means satisfying customer needs, not just meeting specifications in a contract. Analyzing product use may also disclose hidden customers—those who do not use the product themselves, but care very much about how use by others may affect them or other areas of concern, such as the environment, aesthetics of the local community, and so on.

4. **Analyze the means of production**—This is important whether the project involves manufacturing a product, delivering a service, or performing some intellectual or administrative activity. This step, which takes a process view, may clarify or confirm internal customers already identified or add additional internal customers that were missed when analyzing the project team and organization.

Case Study

The concepts of quality management are illuminated by a case study that develops progressively throughout this book. As with the exercise in Chapter 1, readers should take time to complete the case study tasks. Not doing so may limit learning. Reading about something has some value, but actually doing something is far more effective for internalizing new concepts and information for future use. Readers should probably start a case study file or notebook to collect and retain papers associated with task work. The case study subject should be relevant to most readers, given the universal presence of cell phones and laptops in business and society in general.

> **Case Study: Task 1**—Read the case study information in Appendix 1. Identify customers by considering external, internal, and hidden customers. It is not necessary to divide customers into these three categories, but doing so may be helpful to clarify the concept of customers and make sure that identification is as complete as possible.

The result may be a rather long list of perceived customers. It probably should be. If the list is short, the team should go back and reconsider. A short list of key customers may seem convenient for management, but such a list probably includes only the most obvious customers. The intent here is to identify *all* the customers, not just those that come immediately to mind. Customers are important because they have requirements that must be met. If the team does not identify all potential customers, it runs the risk of not identifying all potential requirements. Projects based on incomplete requirements will encounter changes that may confound implementation or even lead to project failure. A list of fifteen, twenty, or even thirty potential customers may seem excessive, but it is the right and necessary place to start. For the purposes of this case study and considering space limitations, we will establish a list of five customers. Your list should have been much longer. The five customers are:

1. State of Dakota
2. Hardware Development Division
3. Users
4. Federal Communications Commission
5. Union of Concerned Citizens

Prioritizing Customers

Not all customers are created equal. An old adage about individual rank in organizations applies here: "If everybody is somebody, nobody is anybody." If all customers are considered equal, the project team may have an impossible task when applying limited project resources during project implementation. The project team must prioritize customers. The purpose is to gain an understanding of the relative importance of the many customers, some of whom may have been identified through enthusiasm of the team during the identification process rather than rational analysis. The purpose is not to identify customers to be ignored or eliminated. The resulting priorities should be a source for reflection. A customer ranked very low in priority may not be a legitimate customer. The team should review that particular customer and determine if it should be removed from the list. Or it may be that the team did not fully consider the potential influence of that customer. In either case, the team should keep in mind that one, single customer may be a showstopper—a customer that can individually cause the project to stop work.

The importance of prioritization demands a rigorous, disciplined process. One such approach is the L-shaped matrix, in which customers are compared to each other on a one-to-one basis (see Figure 4.2).

The first step when applying the L-shaped matrix is to build the matrix by entering the names of the elements to be prioritized along both the vertical and horizontal axes. In Figure 4.2, the letters A, B, C, D, E, and F represent elements to be prioritized.

The next step is to compare the elements to each other on a one-to-one basis to determine importance. First, A in the vertical column on the left is compared to B along the horizontal row to the right, then A to C along the horizontal row, then A to D, and so on. Then B in the vertical column on the left is compared to A along the horizontal row to the right, B to C, B to D, and so on until all elements have been compared to each other. When evaluating the elements, the

	A	B	C	D	E	F	Row Total	Relative Dec. Value
A		5	1	10	1/5	1/5	16.4	0.21
B	1/5		1/5	1	1	5	7.4	0.09
C	1	5		1/5	1/10	5	11.3	0.14
D	1/10	1	5		1/5	1	7.3	0.09
E	5	1	10	5		1/10	21.1	0.26
F	5	1/5	1/5	1	10		16.4	0.21
						Grand Total	79.9	

Key:
10   Much more important
5   More important
1   Equally important
1/5 Less important
1/10 Much less important

Figure 4.2. The L-shaped matrix.

first is always compared to the second. For example, when comparing A on the vertical axis to B on the horizontal axis, we evaluate A against B. If we believe A and B are of equal importance, we enter a score of 1 in the matrix cell. If we believe A is more important than B, we enter a score of 5. If A is much more important than B, we enter a score of 10. If we believe A is less important than B, we enter the inverse of the "more important" score of 5—we enter 1/5. And if A is much less important, we enter a score of 1/10. Each comparison also determines the reverse comparison. If A compared to B is rated as 5, then B compared to A must be rated as 1/5. The team should make both entries in the matrix immediately so that no unintentional inconsistency results. This scoring convention is also shown in Figure 4.2.

After completing the pair-wise comparisons, scores in each row should be added to determine a row total. Now is a convenient time to convert fractional numbers to decimals. Row totals are added to determine a grand total.

The last step is to divide each individual row total by the grand total. The result shows what percentages the row totals represent of the grand total. These relative decimal values indicate priority, the goal of applying the L-shaped matrix technique.

Case Study: Task 2—Using an L-shaped matrix, prioritize your customer list. To reduce time required, limit your list to five customers. Try to select customers from all categories: external, internal, and hidden.

Your completed matrix should look something like Figure 4.3. Notice in Figure 4.3 that Users (not State of Dakota, the paying customer) are rated as highest priority. This is probably a healthy view. State of Dakota may be paying the project bill, but if Users do not like the network, they will not buy the service and the project will be a failure in practice. Notice also that Hardware Development Division, an internal customer, is rated very low in priority. This, too, is probably a healthy view. Project teams, especially the more technical elements, can sometimes focus too much on themselves, forgetting that they only exist to meet some customer requirement.

This completes the first step in a seven-step quality journey that provides a framework for quality management. The framework is not unique to any particular technical domain or industry. It may be applied to any project, anywhere, any time (see Figure 4.4).

Identifying Requirements

Customers are sources of requirements that must be met for project success. The contract awarded by the paying customer is the most obvious source of requirements. Contract terms and conditions prescribe what must be done. Project and organizational elements, including suppliers and subcontractors,

Customer Prioritization	State of Dakota	Hardware Dev Div	Users	FCC	Union of Conc Cit	Row Total	Relative Decimal Value
State of Dakota		10	1/5	1	5	16.2	0.28
Hardware Dev Div	1/10		1/10	1/5	1/5	0.6	0.01
Users	5	10		1/5	5	20.2	0.34
FCC	1	5	5		5	16	0.27
Union of Conc Cit	1/5	5	1/5	1/5		5.6	0.10
					Grand Total	58.6	

Figure 4.3.   L-shaped matrix for customer prioritization.

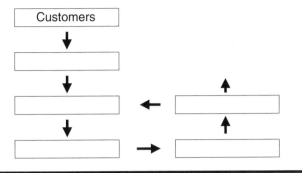

Figure 4.4. Quality journey: customers.

are also sources of requirements. Users and affected groups provide additional requirements, often of great importance to the project team. "Affected groups" are those that participate in product or service delivery in some way, such as warehouses, transportation providers, original equipment manufacturers, and so on. Government agencies and other regulatory agencies are also a source of requirements that must not be overlooked. Last, groups of the concerned provide requirements that must be considered.

Identifying requirements includes defining them in such a way that they are useful to the project team. Requirements are not vague statements of fantasy, but they are generally stated; details come later. A good example of a requirement is "Responsive telephone hotline service." While the precise meaning is lacking, it provides a foundation for further quality planning.

Requirements may be explicitly stated. The contract or government regulations are sources of explicit requirements. Contract requirements may exist in minute design detail or they may be stated as functional requirements that prescribe less detail or performance requirements that simply describe a desired outcome. Requirements may also be implied or unstated. Users, affected groups, and concerned groups may be sources of implied requirements. A user of an off-road vehicle may have a requirement for a CD player, but this user really intends to run the vehicle off-road across some very rough terrain, not just use it for trips to the shopping mall. This user has an implied requirement for a rugged CD player that will withstand extreme use. The common characteristic of all requirements is that they are in some way measurable. If the requirement deals with matters that cannot be measured, the project team will be unable to determine if it has met the requirement.

Defining requirements may require research, interviews, and analysis. Even contract requirements, often negotiated by people not on the project team, may require analysis and interviews with the paying customer to determine and confirm exactly what is required. It is best to involve the whole team in this process. An old Japanese proverb advises that "None of us is as smart as all of us." Involving different people with different views and insights leads to better results than those obtained by one individual.

It is also essential to involve the customer. Customer interviews are useful means for collecting information and are a foundation for analyzing needs and defining requirements. It is helpful to review results with the customers to confirm understanding before proceeding.

Having done all this, the project team should still expect and be prepared to deal with change. Customers can change their minds. New technologies may arise that allow new performance capabilities. Laws may change. New groups of concerned citizens may surface. Requirements definition is an essential and dynamic process.

> **Case Study: Task 3**—Using your prioritized customer list as a base, identify customer requirements. Consider all or several types of customers. Remember that requirements are measurable in some way and generally stated. Do not go into great detail.

Your requirements list will be unique, based on your list of identified customers. For case study purposes, we will consider the following identified requirements:

- Access
- Speed
- Reliability
- Environmentally friendly
- Regulatory compliant

Prioritizing Requirements

As with customers, not all requirements are created equal. A top-priority customer is not necessarily the source of all top-priority requirements. Remember, too, that one, single requirement may be a showstopper. A rigorous method for prioritizing requirements is the Full Analytical Criteria Method.

This is a three-step process that begins with the L-shaped matrix developed to prioritize customer requirements, applies the L-shaped matrix to individual customer requirements, and then combines the results into a single matrix of project priorities. The overall process is summarized in Figure 4.5.

Again, the first step has already been completed. We have prioritized customers using an L-shaped matrix. The next step is to prioritize requirements by comparing requirements to each other from the view of each individual customer. We put ourselves "in the shoes" of each customer and prepare an L-shaped matrix that compares requirements to each other considering the view of that customer. The result is a number of separate matrices equal to the number of customers. This can be a challenge for the project team. Some of the customer-view information may come from interviews, general knowledge of the customer, or just plain brainstorming about how this customer might view the importance of the criteria when compared to each other. Figures 4.6A through 4.6C show the first-step customer prioritization matrix and the five requirements-prioritization matrices developed for our five customers.

The last step is the tricky part. We combine the results of customer prioritization with the several results of requirements prioritization to obtain an integrated prioritization of requirements and customers. We construct this matrix by listing the customers along the horizontal axis and the requirements along the vertical axis. It is helpful to include the customer priority value in the axis listing. We then fill in the values for requirements in each column by multiplying the customer priority value times the requirement value from

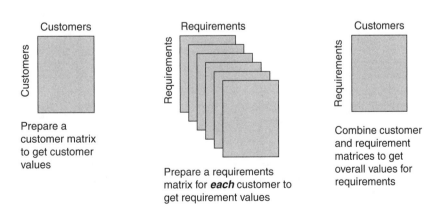

Figure 4.5. Full Analytical Criteria Method.

Customer Prioritization	State of Dakota	Hardware Dev Div	Users	FCC	UCC	Row Total	Relative Decimal Value
State of Dakota		10	0.2	1	5	16.2	0.28
Hardware Dev Div	0.1		0.1	0.2	0.2	0.6	0.01
Users	5	10		0.2	5	20.2	0.34
FCC	1	5	5		5	16.0	0.27
Union of Conc Cit (UCC)	0.2	5	0.2	0.2		5.6	0.10
					Grand Total	58.6	

Requirements Prioritization, State of Dakota View	Access	Speed	Reliability	Enviro-Friendly	Regulatory Compliant	Row Total	Relative Decimal Value
Access		5	1	0.2	0.2	6.4	0.14
Speed	0.2		0.2	0.2	0.2	0.8	0.02
Reliability	1	5		0.2	0.2	6.4	0.14
Environmentally Friendly	5	5	5		1	16.0	0.35
Regulatory Compliant	5	5	5	1		16.0	0.35
					Grand Total	45.6	

Figure 4.6A.   Customer prioritization matrix and requirements prioritization matrix, State of Dakota view.

Requirements Prioritization, Hardware Dev Div View	Access	Speed	Reliability	Enviro-Friendly	Regulatory Compliant	Row Total	Relative Decimal Value
Access		5	1	10	1	17.0	0.32
Speed	0.2		0.2	10	1	11.4	0.21
Reliability	1	5		10	1	17.0	0.32
Environmentally Friendly	0.1	0.1	0.1		0.2	0.5	0.01
Regulatory Compliant	1	1	1	5		8.0	0.15
					Grand Total	53.9	

Requirements Prioritization, Users View	Access	Speed	Reliability	Enviro-Friendly	Regulatory Compliant	Row Total	Relative Decimal Value
Access		5	1	5	1	12.0	0.31
Speed	0.2		0.2	5	1	6.4	0.16
Reliability	1	5		5	1	12.0	0.31
Environmentally Friendly	0.2	0.2	0.2		0.2	0.8	0.02
Regulatory Compliant	1	1	1	5		8.0	0.20
					Grand Total	39.2	

Figure 4.6B.   Requirements prioritization matrices, hardware development division and users views.

Requirements Prioritization, FCC View	Access	Speed	Reliability	Enviro-Friendly	Regulatory Compliant	Row Total	Relative Decimal Value
Access		1	1	1	0.1	3.1	0.06
Speed	1		1	1	0.1	3.1	0.06
Reliability	1	1		1	0.1	3.1	0.06
Environmentally Friendly	1	1	1		0.1	3.1	0.06
Regulatory Compliant	10	10	10	10		40.0	0.76
					Grand Total	52.4	

Requirements Prioritization, UCC View	Access	Speed	Reliability	Enviro-Friendly	Regulatory Compliant	Row Total	Relative Decimal Value
Access		1	1	0.1	0.2	2.3	0.04
Speed	1		1	0.1	0.2	2.3	0.04
Reliability	1	1		0.1	0.2	2.3	0.04
Environmentally Friendly	10	10	10		5	35.0	0.61
Regulatory Compliant	5	5	5	0.2		15.2	0.27
					Grand Total	57.1	

Figure 4.6C.   Requirements prioritization matrices, FCC and UCC views.

the requirements prioritization matrix for that customer's view. Figure 4.7A shows the calculation method and Figure 4.7B shows the resulting integrated matrix entitled "Customer-Weighted Requirements Prioritization."

The matrix shows that, by a significant margin, the highest priority for the Dakota Wireless Network is to be regulatory compliant. This may not have been our intuitive choice, but it makes great sense. We can design and build the best wireless system in the universe, but if it does not meet regulatory requirements, we can never turn it on.

Quality Planning and Project Planning

It is essential that these steps of customer and requirement prioritization be completed early in the project, before the project plan or project design has been completed. Not doing so may result in a project plan that takes you someplace you did not want to go. This completes the second step in the quality journey (see Figure 4.8).

Identifying Standards

Standards may be viewed in two ways. In the traditional view, a standard is a prescribed way of doing something. Standards have also been viewed by some as explicit targets to be met or quantifiable definitions of generally stated requirements. In the traditional view, explicit targets are specifications, not standards. This discussion adheres to the traditional view, recognizing that identifying both standards and specifications is part of quality planning. Metrics are closely linked to standards and specifications. Metrics are a means of measurement for determining the degree of conformance to specifications. They will be discussed under quality assurance.

Standards guide project implementation. They describe how the project team should or must employ processes. Many sources exist for consideration by the project team. ISO standards such as the ISO 9000-series (quality management) or the ISO 14000-series (environmental management) should be considered if they are not already required by the contract. ANSI national standards constitute a wide-ranging collection of standards that may apply. The *PMBOK® Guide* is recognized as an ANSI national standard for project management. Standards published by IEEE and other professional organizations may be required or useful. Finally, organizations may have codified their own standards—ways of doing things that are proven and mandatory for use.

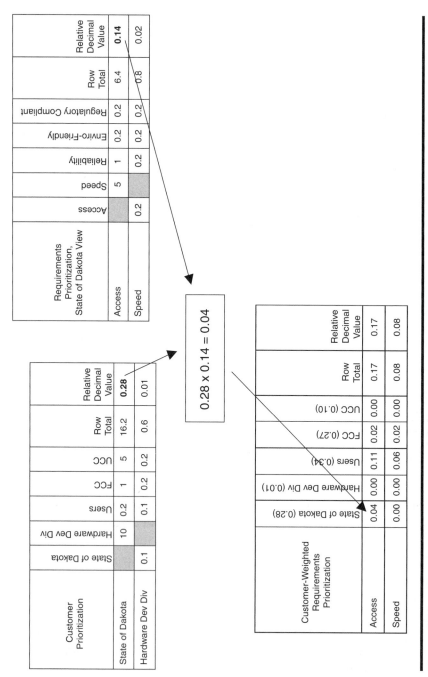

Figure 4.7A. Creating a customer-weighted requirements prioritization matrix.

Customer-Weighted Requirements Prioritization	State of Dakota (0.28)	Hardware Dev Div (0.01)	Users (0.34)	FCC (0.27)	UCC (0.10)	Row Total	Relative Decimal Value
Access	0.04	0.00	0.11	0.02	0.00	0.17	0.17
Speed	0.00	0.00	0.06	0.02	0.00	0.08	0.08
Reliability	0.04	0.00	0.11	0.02	0.00	0.17	0.17
Environmentally Friendly	0.10	0.00	0.01	0.02	0.06	0.18	0.18
Regulatory Compliant	0.10	0.00	0.07	0.21	0.03	0.40	0.40
					Grand Total	1.0	

Figure 4.7B. Customer-weighted requirements prioritization matrix.

Specifications are the further detailing of requirements. Requirements are generally stated; specifications are exact—they are specific and measurable. Consider the previous example of a requirement: "Responsive telephone hotline service." A specification for this requirement might be: "Answer 99 percent of hotline service calls within one ring." Progressing from requirements to specifications is an important step that may not be easy. Operational definitions provide the link.

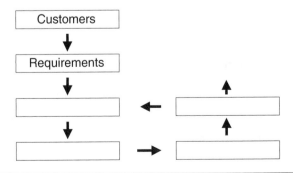

Figure 4.8. Quality journey: requirements.

Operational definitions describe what something is and how it is measured. They are a formal way of answering the question "What do you mean by that?" Both Deming and Juran emphasized the importance of operational definitions in their work. Here are two examples:

1. **"Responsive" telephone hotline service**—The amount of time before a call is answered expressed as the number of rings as measured by the automated telephone data system.
2. **"Hot" coffee**—The temperature of the coffee as measured by a standard Fahrenheit thermometer after standing in a Styrofoam cup for three minutes in a room with ambient temperature of no less than sixty-eight degrees.

Both of these operational definitions provide clarification of ambiguous terms—"responsive" and "hot"—and allow the project team to develop specifications by rational analysis rather than guesswork.

Moving from requirements to specifications is a three-step process:

1. Identify a requirement.
2. Develop an operational definition.
3. Develop a specific value against which performance will be measured to determine success.

Specifications may be provided by the paying customer in the contract or provided by other customers informally. Even specifications in the contract may require customer coordination to ensure understanding by all project participants.

> **Case Study: Task 4**—Select two requirements from your list and develop operational definitions of terms. Then develop specifications for the requirements.

This completes the third step in the quality journey (see Figure 4.9). Standards and specifications are the end of quality planning and the foundation for quality assurance and control.

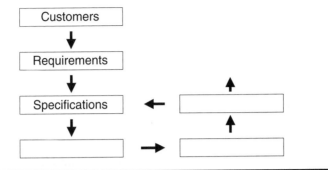

Figure 4.9. Quality journey: specifications.

Example Case: Quality Planning

Preparing high-resolution graphics for a national conference.

Situation

Technical Services Company (TSC) is working for a large government organization under a time-and-materials contract. The contract defines several areas of endeavor, with specific work directed through individual delivery orders that specify scope and not-to-exceed levels of funding for labor and materials.

The government organization ("the client") intends to participate in a national technical conference by sponsoring a booth that will tout its achievements in the technical focus area of the conference. They do not have the internal capability to produce the necessary materials for the booth, so they issued a delivery order to TSC to produce, among other things, large-scale high-resolution full-color graphics.

As is typical practice under this contract, the TSC Project Manager worked with the client Project Manager to define the terms of the delivery order. The client retrains final decision authority for all details, but both parties have found that collaborative definition works best and avoids unexpected overruns downstream.

The TSC PM knows this is risky business. The client does not have a well-settled view of what is desired. And it is likely that the process of refining the requirements may suggest new requirements that were not anticipated. He also knows that good definition of requirements and specifications is an essential element of good quality planning. TSC can do the design work, but printing the final product requires specialized equipment. TSC will outsource the printing to a local company.

To aid in final specification definition, the TSC PM has established the capability to produce small-scale low-resolution black-and-white mock-ups of the graphics. This will allow the client to see what the final result might be and allow multiple iterations of modified designs at a reasonable cost.

After several weeks of coordination, suggestions, mock-ups, and review, TSC and the client agreed on final specifications. The TSC PM gave the client one final look at the design, then printed and delivered the final product. A few days later, the client PM called and asked if she could make a couple of changes. She apologized profusely, but indicated that the changes were really important. The TSC PM determined that there was sufficient funding remaining on the delivery order to change and re-run the work. He did so and delivered the revised product.

The next day, the client PM called the TSC PM. This time she was more agitated. She said her boss had seen the TSC graphics and didn't like them. She said he "needed to get over here right now and correct the unacceptable work." The TSC PM knew that funds on the delivery order had been exhausted. TSC had a right in the contract to require the client to add additional funds to accomplish the work. However, the client's contracting officer had seen too many requests for additional funding and was getting a bit out of sorts. To avoid potential adverse effects on the relationship, TSC made a business decision to make the desired changes at their own expense.

Analysis

This is not an unusual situation. Clients don't always know what they want. They often depend on the expertise of the contractor to define what is possible within current technology. In this case, the TSC PM did the right thing in using cheaper mock-ups to refine requirements. At the same time, the ease of change using the mock-ups may have lulled the client into a false sense of security. Since it was so easy to make changes to the mock-up, the client may not have fully appreciated the huge expense of making changes to the final product. The TSC PM's willingness to make the first change (within funds) may have exacerbated this feeling. Perhaps the TSC PM should have spent more time explaining the financial implications of the change.

There is another part of this story that goes beyond the scope of the delivery order. It has to do with the organizational culture or ways of doing business. In spite of the TSC PM's efforts at collaborative development of requirements, it appears that the client PM never took the results to the boss for review and approval. There are many possible reasons for this—over confidence, past criticism, the boss was too busy—but whatever the reason, internal coordination was not complete.

The relationship with the contracting officer is the third influential element. Under a time-and-materials contract, TSC is not required to deliver a specific product. They are only required to deliver their "best effort" at producing that product. If funds are exhausted before the product is complete, the client has two choices: accept the product at the current level of completion, or add funding sufficient to complete the work. The contracting officer had seen too many requests for additional funding. Each one required a modification to the delivery order, which meant additional—and in her view, unnecessary—work for the contract office staff. While both parties had some responsibility for these situations, the contracting officer tended to blame TSC for bad management. She expected TSC to complete work within available funds. After all, TSC participated in preparing the estimates. She may also have been critical of the government PMs, resulting in a reluctance on their part to go to her for delivery order modifications. Regardless of where the blame may lie, TSC chose to complete the work using their own funding and avoid any unpleasantness with the contracting officer.

Lessons Learned

1. Quality planning is important and has far-reaching effects on project performance.
2. In project performance changes made early (during planning) are less expensive than changes made later (during implementation).
3. Quality planning may involve cultural, social, or other factors in addition to technical factors.

Summary

◆ Quality management includes quality planning, quality assurance, quality control, and quality improvement.

- The quality management plan is part of the project plan. It includes the quality policy (intended direction of the organization regarding quality) and answers the questions: Who is in charge? (infrastructure and responsibilities), Where are we going? (goals), and How are we going to get there? (processes).
- Quality planning is the process of identifying quality requirements and/or standards for the project and its deliverables and documenting how the project will demonstrate compliance with quality requirements.
- Quality planning is the foundation that allows quality to be planned in, not inspected in.
- Customers are the base in project quality. They may be classified as external, internal, or hidden.
- Identifying customers is the first step in a seven-step quality journey that provides a general framework for quality management. Customers may be prioritized using an L-shaped matrix.
- Identifying requirements is the second step in the quality journey. Requirements may be prioritized using the Full Analytical Criteria Method.
- Customer and requirement identification and prioritization should be performed early in project planning so the project starts in the right direction.
- Identifying specifications is the third step in the quality journey. Specifications are specific and measurable statements of requirements.
- Operational definitions provide a link between requirements and specifications. Operational definitions remove ambiguity of terms by describing what something is and how it is measured.
- Standards are closely related to specifications. Standards address how something is to be done. Specifications provide specific targets for performance.

Points to Ponder

1. Name the four elements of quality management. Explain how they relate to each other and why each one is important.
2. Describe the purpose of a quality management plan. Describe the basic elements of a good plan.
3. From your personal knowledge or experience, give or create several examples of quality policy statements. Explain the strengths or possible weaknesses of each one.

4. What is the role of customers in quality planning? Why are they important? Should they be prioritized? If so, how important is the final priority ranking?
5. Discuss the role of requirements in quality planning. Include the issue of prioritization.
6. What is the role of standards in quality planning? From your personal knowledge or experience, describe several existing standards that might come into play when managing various kinds of projects.
7. What is the role of specifications in quality planning? How do operational definitions link specifications to requirements?
8. From your personal knowledge or experience, develop at least three operational definitions and describe how they might be used to link requirements and specifications.

Exercise

a. From your personal experience, select a product (goods or services) that you know something about. Develop a list of at least five customers that might be associated with the product. Prioritize the customers using an L-Shaped Matrix.
b. Now develop a list of at least five requirements that might be associated with the product. Prioritize them using the Full Analytical Criteria Method. Be sure to finish with the Customer-Weighted Prioritization Matrix.
c. Present the results in class or to a collaborative work group.

References

1. *A Guide to the Project Management Body of Knowledge—Fifth Edition*, Project Management Institute, Newtown Square, PA, 2013, p. 227.
2. Ibid., p. 227.
3. Ibid., p. 557.

5

Project Quality Assurance

"Quality assurance" can be a troublesome term because it has distinctly different meanings to different people. Recall that Joseph Juran did not include quality assurance in his Juran Trilogy of quality planning, quality control, and quality improvement. In Juran's view, quality assurance is similar to quality control, but performed by other people. Quality control is performed by those directly responsible for producing a product. Quality assurance is performed by people external to the production process who have a need to know about the quality of the product. For example, inspecting an item for conformance to requirements at the end of a production line is quality control. Inspecting a purchased item for conformance to requirements on the loading dock is quality assurance. This view, when taken through the lens of a project context, may suggest that quality assurance and quality control are the same. During the planning process, project teams may encounter make-or-buy decisions. A project requirement might be met by in-house performance using internal resources and capabilities (make). It might also be met by purchasing a finished product from an outside source through contract (buy). Either way, the project team is responsible for ultimate conformance to requirements. Whether that conformance is checked at the end of an internal production process or at delivery of an externally produced product, it is still—in the eyes of the project team—quality control.

The *PMBOK® Guide—Fifth Edition* defines its Perform Quality Assurance process as "... the process of auditing the quality requirements and the results from quality control measures to ensure that appropriate quality standards and operational definitions are used."[1] This is a departure from—or perhaps an evolution of—the definition in the *Third Edition* that stated quality assurance was "... the application of planned, systematic quality activities to ensure that the project will employ all processes needed to meet requirements."[2] This earlier definition offered a logical follow-on to quality planning. The new definition seems to suggest a somewhat independent process of auditing that mixes in results from quality control activities. This co-mingling of quality assurance and quality control creates a conundrum for project managers: if both quality assurance and quality control use measurement and analysis of project performance, what is the difference between the two?

This "troublesome term" aspect is not trivial. It may be inherent in the nature of the process. Quality assurance may be viewed as a borderline activity —a bridge or link—between quality planning and quality control. In one sense, it looks back to planning and might be folded into planning as a final step. In another sense, it looks forward to control and might be folded into quality control as a precursor or initial step. Folding quality assurance into other processes as a sub-element may well reduce its overall relevance. To be effective, quality assurance must have a clear and reasonable definition that establishes its unique role and sets it apart from other processes.

Beyond technical definition issues, there is a more social issue in play: language usage. Often, "quality assurance" is used in conversation and writing when the term "quality control" would be more accurate and more properly applied. This may be because people are not well informed about the difference between the two. Or, assuming equivalent meaning, people consider "assurance" to be a nicer, less offensive word than "control," which may have strongly negative, personal associations. It is not uncommon to hear something like the following in the project work area: "Who's going to QA that before it goes to the client?" The intent of the question is to determine who will review a product for completeness and correctness before delivering it to the client. A more accurate question would be, "Who's going to QC that before it goes to the client?" Whatever the reason for possible confusion, the project team must understand the difference between assurance and control. Both are essential elements of quality management and both are necessary for project success.

Briefly, quality assurance addresses the methods; it is the combined set of activities that the project team will perform to meet project objectives. Quality control addresses the outcomes; it is monitoring performance and doing something about the results. Quality control will be addressed in Chapter 6.

Quality Assurance

ISO 9000 defines quality assurance as the "part of quality management focused on providing confidence that quality requirements will be fulfilled."[3] This broad, international consensus definition opens the door to quality assurance as a separate element of quality management. Translating it into a project context yields *providing confidence that project performance will conform to project requirements*. Still, a "how-to" element is missing. The "part of quality management" element of the ISO definition may be refined—within the spirit and intent of the ISO standard—to read *defined activities*. The result describes a unique process that stands apart from the other processes in quality management. Quality assurance is the set of defined activities that provide confidence that project performance will conform to project requirements. Quality assurance activities are the things the project team will do to check project performance against the project plan using specifications as the targets.

Developing Assurance Activities

Developing assurance activities involves more than delegation. Coherent, integrated activities arise from a disciplined process of steps:

1. Select the relevant standard or specification.
2. Using operational definitions, define an activity that will collect data and compare results to the plan. Develop and apply metrics (discussed below).
3. Define and provide resources.
4. Assign responsibility to a specific entity.
5. Assemble activities into a quality assurance plan.

Metrics

Recall that metrics are a means of measurement to determine the degree of conformance to specifications. They close the loop and link together requirements, specifications, assurance activities, and the metrics themselves. See the examples below.

◆ **Requirement** (generally stated)—"Responsive telephone hotline service."

◆ **Specification** (specific and measurable)—"Answer 99 percent of hot-line service calls within one ring."
◆ **Assurance activity** (action to be taken)—Determine percentage of calls answered on one ring during a forty-eight-hour period.
◆ **Metric** (means of measurement)—Percentage of calls answered on one ring.

> **Case Study: Task 5**—Using the two specifications developed in the last task, develop an assurance activity for each. Develop more than one activity for each specification if necessary.

Review your assurance activities and compare them to the development steps described above.

◆ Are they based on a specification?
◆ Are they based on an operational definition that states what a performance target is and how it is measured?
◆ Are necessary resources identified?
◆ Has responsibility been assigned to a specific entity?

This completes the fourth step in the quality journey (see Figure 5.1).

Quality Assurance Plan

In a project consisting of several hundred or even several thousand tasks, quality assurance activities can be difficult to track. They should be assembled

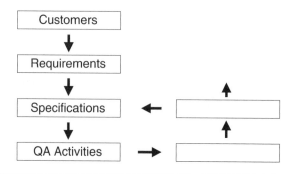

Figure 5.1. Quality journey: quality assurance activities.

into a quality assurance plan that documents all activities and allows effective management. Mature organizations may have a prescribed format for quality assurance plans. If not, the project team will have to develop one. A quality assurance plan should include at least the following elements:

◆ The work breakdown structure reference number for the task concerned
◆ A statement of the requirement (usually from the customer)
◆ A statement of the specification that is specific and measurable
◆ A description of the assurance activity (what is to be done)
◆ Schedule information (when it is to be done)
◆ Designation of the responsible entity (who will do it)

A simple format for quality assurance plans is shown in Figure 5.2.

> **Case Study: Task 6A**—Select some aspect of your own work and prepare a one-line entry in the quality assurance plan format shown in Figure 5.2. Be specific about what will be done, when it will be done, and who will do it.
>
> **Case Study: Task 6B**—Now that you have some experience in a familiar domain, return to the Dakota Wireless Network case study and, considering all the elements developed to this point, make a one-line entry in the quality assurance plan format shown in Figure 5.2.

Quality Audits

The primary mechanism for determining the effectiveness of quality assurance activities is the quality audit. Any audit is a structured review of

WBS Ref	Requirement	Specification	Assurance Activity	Schedule	Responsible Entity
	(from customer)	(specific and measurable)	(what is to be done)	(when it will be done)	(who will do it)

Figure 5.2.   Quality assurance plan.

performance against the plan. The *PMBOK® Guide* defines a quality audit as "... a structured, independent process to determine if project activities comply with organizational and project policies, processes, and procedures."[4] The audit may use results obtained from quality control to determine if quality assurance activities are having the desired result. If results do not show conformance to specification, quality assurance activities should be reviewed and improved.

Quality assurance audits may be conducted on a scheduled basis (for instance, at the completion of major milestones) or may be conducted at random (for instance, only if quality control results exceed certain thresholds or the boss decides to initiate an audit out of the blue).

Quality assurance audits may be conducted by internal or external elements. A dedicated, honest project team may have no difficulty conducting an internal audit, but beyond the honesty issue, project team members may be just too close to things to get an accurate picture. External audits often provide more objective results and are often more respected by third parties, such as higher level management.

Interest in quality audits increased significantly with the publication of the ISO 9000-series quality management standards. The *ISO 9001* standard was heavily focused on documentation. So much so that a mildly derisive comment arose that in an ISO quality management system, it didn't matter what you did as long as you documented it. The 2008 edition of *ISO 9001* decreased the focus on documentation and increased the focus on the results of the quality management system, which is as it should be.

The emphasis on audits in the ISO 9000-series standards gave rise to a cottage industry—perhaps even a guild—of quality auditors. These were people who were specially prepared and even certified by a third-party organization to conduct quality audits. For a fee, they would come into an organization and quickly conduct a comprehensive audit that would meet ISO requirements and provide the organization with helpful information. The view, strongly espoused by the auditors, was that these experts were uniquely able to audit quality management systems. Even considering that external auditors may be uniquely unbiased, there is no reason why an organization cannot conduct an effective internal audit as long as everyone agrees up front to let the chips fall where they may—to accept the results as they are determined—without cover-up or punitive response.

This completes the fifth step in the quality journey (see Figure 5.3).

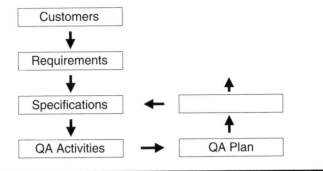

Figure 5.3. Quality journey: quality assurance plan.

Example Case: Quality Assurance

Building a bridge.

Situation

Coleman Construction Company was awarded a contract by a local munici-
pality to replace a small bridge over a waterway in the downtown area. The
bridge was historically significant. The city requirements called for specific
design criteria, to include four decorative lampposts, one on each corner of
the bridge. The lampposts were to be mounted on concrete foundations by
four large bolts that would be set in the concrete, pass through matching
holes in the base plates of the lamp posts, and be secured by large nuts con-
cealed by a decorative cover.

Because of the historical significance, a grand opening was scheduled,
complete with bands, official speakers of note, and festive decorations. Final
installation was a simple matter. The lampposts would be lowered in place
and secured beginning at 9:00 a.m. with the commemorative events to begin
promptly at 11:00 a.m.

On the day of dedication, everything was ready. Decorations were in place,
the bands were assembling, and local officials were glad-handing the arriv-
ing crowd. In the background, a Coleman crane lifted the first lamppost into
place. The lamppost rose above the concrete foundation and slowly settled
over the bolts. Almost, that is. When the base plate met the bolts, it stopped.
An engineer quickly moved forward to guide the plate over the bolts, but
he could not make a match. He pushed forward, he pushed to the right, he

pushed to the left ... all to no avail. It seemed the holes in the base plate did not match the placement of the bolts in the foundation.

Without the lampposts, the bridge could not be opened for traffic. The event was called off and the lampposts were returned to the shop for new base plates that matched the configuration of the bolts in the foundations. The lampposts were subsequently installed without incident and the bridge was opened without ceremony.

Analysis

This was a clear failure of quality assurance. The task was a familiar task. Coleman had constructed hundreds of bridges. This was a no-brainer. It was a routine project. Perhaps it was too routine. Perhaps the project team made too many assumptions about how things would proceed. Perhaps they assumed that good things would happen all by themselves.

Good things don't happen by themselves. People have to make good things happen. Here is what the Coleman project manager could have done, but apparently didn't:

1. Issue the same design specifications to the foundation designers and the base plate designers.
2. Check the completed designs to make sure the configuration of the bolts matched the configuration of the holes in the base plate.
3. Check the materials obtained to make sure the bolts were the right length, the right diameter, and the right grade. Make sure the nuts match the bolts.
4. Check installation of the bolts in the foundation to make sure it matches design.
5. Check fabrication of the base plates to make sure they match design.
6. Do a rehearsal. Run through an installation before the big event to make sure there are no unanticipated problems.

A good quality assurance plan would have defined activities similar to these and assigned responsibility for accomplishing them. A good quality assurance plan would have provided confidence that project performance met project requirements. A good quality assurance plan would have prevented a thoroughly embarrassing situation.

Lessons Learned

1. Quality assurance activities provide checks on project performance.
2. Quality assurance plans provide a disciplined means of aligning project performance with project requirements.
3. Quality assurance plans can prevent project failure.

Summary

◆ Quality assurance is a set of defined activities that provide confidence that project performance will conform to project requirements.

◆ Quality assurance addresses the methods; it is the combined set of activities that the project team will perform to meet project objectives. Quality control addresses the outcomes; it is about monitoring performance and doing something about the results.

◆ Defining quality assurance activities is the fourth step in a seven-step quality journey that provides a general framework for quality management.

◆ Quality assurance activities are based on specifications and operational definitions. They include identified resources and responsible entities.

◆ Metrics are the means of measurement that link requirements, specifications, assurance activities, and the metrics themselves.

◆ The quality assurance plan lists all assurance activities in one place to assist in managing project quality.

◆ Preparing a quality assurance plan is the fifth step in the quality journey.

◆ Quality audits are structured reviews of the quality system. They may be scheduled or random and conducted by internal or external elements.

Points to Ponder

1. Explain why quality assurance must stand alone as a separate element of quality management.
2. How does quality assurance serve as a link between quality planning and quality control?
3. What is the role of quality assurance activities? Describe the process for defining activities.

4. Why are quality metrics important? What is their role? How are they developed?
5. Discuss the purpose of a quality assurance plan. Describe the various elements and explain their importance.
6. How do quality audits contribute to overall quality management? What are the advantages or disadvantages of internal and external audits?

Exercise

a. Choose a product or activity about which you have some personal knowledge. An activity may be something simple like a party, sports event, concert, or vacation. Sketch out the requirements for producing a successful product or conducting a successful activity. Now, develop appropriate quality assurance activities and prepare a quality assurance plan.
b. Present your results in class or to a collaborative work group.

References

1. *A Guide to the Project Management Body of Knowledge—Fifth Edition*, Project Management Institute, Newtown Square, PA, 2013, p. 242.
2. *A Guide to the Project Management Body of Knowledge—Third Edition*, Project Management Institute, Newtown Square, PA, 2004, p. 187.
3. *ISO 9000:2005, Quality management systems—Fundamental and vocabulary*, International Organization for Standardization, Geneva, 2005, p. 7.
4. *A Guide to the Project Management Body of Knowledge—Fifth Edition*, Project Management Institute, Newtown Square, PA, 2013, p. 247.

6

Project Quality Control and Quality Improvement

The *PMBOK® Guide* defines quality control as "The process of monitoring and recording results of executing the quality activities to assess performance and recommend necessary changes."[1] This is an action process in which the project team looks at results and determines necessary corrective action.

Quality Control

Monitoring specific project results serves several important purposes:

◆ Results may confirm that all is well. If results are within specifications (no variance from specifications is indicated), the project team knows that performance is proceeding according to plan.

◆ Results may provide the basis for corrective action. If results do not conform to specifications (some degree of variance is indicated), the project team knows that something has gone wrong or is going wrong. The project team must take corrective action to fix the existing variance from the plan. The team must also identify the source of the variance and take corrective action to prevent it from recurring.

◆ Results provide feedback to the quality assurance process. Results obtained during quality control provide data that are examined during quality audits. Performance that does not conform to specifications indicates that the quality assurance activities associated with that performance are not having the desired effect. Quality assurance activities are intended to ensure conforming performance. If they do not, the project team must analyze the data, determine the shortcoming, improve the quality assurance activities, and update the quality assurance plan.

Role of Inspection

A continuing theme in quality management is that quality is *planned* in, not *inspected* in. Superficially, this may suggest that planning is in; inspection is out. Not true. Inspection plays a significant role in quality management, but it is a role that is different from that in the traditional approach to quality. Products must be inspected at the end of a process to ensure that they conform to specification. Products must be checked before they are delivered to the paying customer. In the traditional approach to quality, as explained earlier, this end-of-process inspection was the principal focus. Results of the inspection allowed delivery of the product or required rework or discard of the defective items.

In the contemporary view of quality, inspection plays a very broad role across and throughout the process. Small, frequent inspections ensure that the process is performing as planned, with the result being fewer nonconforming products at the end of the process. In-process inspection may reveal deficiencies that can be corrected before they cause costly scrap and rework.

Inspections may include several kinds of activities, such as:

- ♦ Measuring physical characteristics of products
- ♦ Examining products for completeness or correct assembly
- ♦ Testing products for performance

Quality Control Tools

Many quality control tools are available to the project team. Ishikawa's seven basic tools are a comprehensive set, but many others exist beyond these. Quality control may be a simple matter of checking something. It may involve the application of complex tools that require some expertise. Many of the tools of quality control are also tools of quality improvement. Their use, their *correct* use, is so important to the project team that they will be addressed separately in Section III.

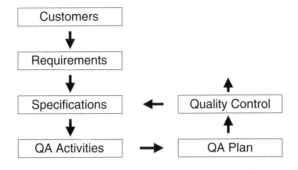

Figure 6.1. Quality journey: quality control.

This completes the sixth step in the quality journey (see Figure 6.1). Note that this step of the journey leads back to a previous step, specifications. Quality control is a process that monitors specific project results to ensure that results conform to specifications.

Quality Improvement

The loop from quality control back to specifications is not the end of the quality journey, however. Figure 6.1 shows another exit from the quality control step. That path goes to quality improvement. Juran defines quality improvement as a "breakthrough ... the organized creation of beneficial change and the attainment of unprecedented levels of performance."[2] Quality improvement is a deliberate process that uses objective measurement and data. All quality improvement begins with data collection. The Japanese word *kaizen* (meaning continual, incremental improvement) is widely used in quality-related activities.

Reasons for Quality Improvement

Quality improvement is not just a good idea. Many practical reasons exist, demanding that organizations continually improve their quality of product or service.

- ◆ A basic reason is to improve products or reduce deficiencies. Better products or fewer deficiencies will improve customer satisfaction, improve reputation, and increase competitiveness.

- Recall that products are not things unto themselves; they meet some kind of customer need. Another reason for quality improvement is to produce better products for customers. This, too, will increase customer satisfaction and may increase deliveries to existing customers and generate sales to new customers.

- Better processes may result in more efficient use of time, less waste, or fewer defects.

- Customers can be a frustrating lot. Give them what they want and they ask for more. Dynamic customer needs and requirements demand that we continually improve to meet the new needs and requirements. We should welcome this attribute of customers. Without it, we might tend to be satisfied with current products and performance and be overtaken, even overcome, by competitors with newer, better ideas.

- Quality improvement may reduce costs. Lower costs can increase competitiveness through lower prices or result in delivery of more product or service for the existing price.

- Global competition is a cold, hard fact of business life. Almost all products or services are subject to competition from just about anyplace in the world. Often, global competitors have an advantage in price because of local labor costs. Quality improvement can make products more competitive in the face of low-cost labor markets.

- New technologies and the pace of technology development require change and enable quality improvement. We must improve to keep up, and the continual changes allow us to improve continually and provide better products and services to our customers.

Quality improvement is a matter of business survival. Consider all the reasons described above. Ignoring any one of them may result in business failure.

Hurdles

If quality improvement is so critical, everyone should support it, but that is not always the case. Quality improvement can be difficult for many reasons. Members of the project team may be disillusioned by past failures. Past efforts at improvement may not have produced any results, or at least not the results that the team expected or considered to be worth the effort.

Members of the team or members of external management may believe, wrongly, that improved quality costs more. They can focus on short-term costs rather than long-term benefits. This can be a difficult mind-set to break, but it must be broken. A focus on short-term costs and a belief that better quality costs more will have devastating effects on the project, the product of the project, customer satisfaction, and the organization as a whole.

Quality improvement responsibility can be delegated down the project team, sometimes to the point where the person responsible has no authority or ability to take effective action. An action passed is not an action completed; it is just an action passed to someone else with uncertain result. The project manager is responsible for project quality. Quality improvement, because of its system orientation, is a responsibility of top management.

Employees are often apprehensive about quality improvement because improvement is *change*. Resistance to change, fear of the unknown, comfort with the status quo—all combine to make quality improvement not something to be assumed, but something to be approached very carefully. Appendix 4 provides additional information on organizational change management.

Improvement Methodology

The plan-do-check-act cycle is a proven, disciplined approach to quality improvement. It was developed by Walter Shewhart and described in his 1939 book, *Statistical Method from the Viewpoint of Quality Control.* Deming and others applied it as the "Shewhart cycle." In Japan, it is known as the "Deming cycle" because Dr. Deming introduced it in his lectures to the Japanese Union of Scientists and Engineers in 1950. The cycle is shown in Figure 6.2. Applying the model is rather straightforward, but not intuitive. It bears some explanation.

◆ **Plan**—This is the starting point. Select a process for improvement. It may be the process that suggests the greatest payback, or the process that suggests the greatest opportunity for success, or the process the boss wants. Initially, it may be beneficial to select a process that shows the greatest potential for successful improvement, maybe the "easiest" one. The team will have less difficulty working through the model the first time, and both the team and management will be encouraged by success. After selecting the right process, analyze it and plan a change that will have beneficial effect.

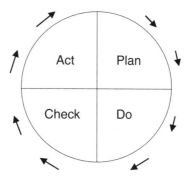

Figure 6.2.   The plan-do-check-act cycle.

◆ **Do**—Apply the change on a small scale, a test case. This is a critical step and the hallmark of the approach. Do not announce the plan as a mandatory change across the entire system. That can lead to "knee-jerking" the work force. If the plan does not have the desired effect, or even makes things worse, the project team and management may lose confidence in the model and perhaps in those who tried to apply it. Both results can be fatal to further quality improvement.

◆ **Check**—Observe the effects of the change. This is more than casual observation. It is a careful and comprehensive study of the results. The project team must fully understand the effects of the change, why they occurred, and how they might affect some other process in the system. This analysis is so important that Dr. Deming changed the title to "study" later in life. Some quality literature describes a plan-do-study-act cycle.

◆ **Act**—If the results are as expected (if they show the intended beneficial effect), implement the change system-wide. The test case shows that the change will probably work as planned, so there is little risk of knee-jerking the work force. Then, because this is a cycle supporting continual improvement, move on to the next aspect of the process or another process that might be the basis for a beneficial change and start the cycle again. If the results are not as expected, move forward in the cycle to the *plan* step and revisit the process to analyze it again and prepare a new plan. This new plan will be based on better information, knowledge about what did not work.

This completes the last step in the quality journey (see Figure 6.3). The quality journey provides a framework for project quality management. Its seven

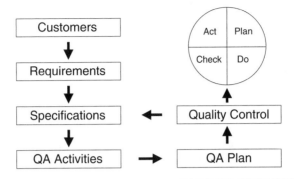

Figure 6.3.   Quality journey: quality improvement.

steps prescribe specific things that project managers and project teams can do to manage quality in their projects. While some projects may have do-main-unique quality considerations and techniques, the framework is fundamentally applicable to any project in any domain. Project managers need never again ask "What am I supposed to do?" regarding quality. The framework shows the way.

Example Case: Quality Control

Telling the story.

Situation

Technical Services Company (TSC) is working for a large government organization under a time-and-materials contract. The government organization ("the client") recently completed a multi-year project in which they accomplished the conversion of a major government facility to a similar facility for local public use. In so doing, they developed and applied many innovative approaches and techniques that would well serve other organizations facing a similar challenge. The government organization issued a delivery order under the TSC contract to capture and document the challenges, methods, and lessons learned and to prepare a booklet describing all of this in a way that might be used as a helpful guide to other organizations.

TSC assigned one of their best engineers to the job. He had a strong technical background, had worked on several of the conversion project tasks under other delivery orders, and had recently completed a Ph.D. program in which he demonstrated consummate writing skills. He was the right person for the job.

Over a period of about eight months, the TSC engineer conducted interviews with key players, researched historical documents and records, and analyzed the collective information. He wrote a comprehensive text with full-color graphics and photos. This was a first-ever product for both TSC and the client. TSC was pleased with their work and was certain the client would be too. TSC delivered the final product with an expectation of *kudos* for their work.

A few days later, the client chief executive called the TSC site manager over to his office. He laid the finished product on his desk and said that he had never seen a product so bad. It was not just a matter of a few glitches, the entire product was unacceptable for delivery. He directed the TSC site manager to fix it and fix it soon.

The TSC site manager and the entire TSC team were stunned by this event. They were also very concerned about cost. The original effort had almost exhausted available funding on the delivery order and they were afraid that the client would require them to produce an acceptable product at their own expense. By coincidence, the TSC site manager had taken a call that morning from someone looking for a job. The manager had expressed mild interest and asked that the caller send over a résumé. The caller had described his experience, which was not engineering related, but he had a strong record of publications in noted journals. He was a good writer. The manager called him back and asked that he come in the next day for an interview. He hired him on the spot.

The new hire was given two tasks: fix the defective product, and do so in a way that showed early results that would convince the client to add additional funding to complete the work. He did both. Within a month, TSC delivered a new product that earned the client's praise for the new product and forgiveness for the earlier misstep.

Analysis

What went wrong here? Most of the TSC staff was not talking. The manager was a very level-headed person who had some quality management experience. He was very open with the new hire. He thought that TSC had a good quality control process and was somewhat mystified as to why things went wrong.

The new hire also had some quality management experience. He determined that TSC did not have a complete quality management system in place. There was no quality planning and no quality assurance, only quality control. In his experience, this was not unusual in organizations like TSC. They tend to be so focused on "getting to work" and billing work hours to the client, that they overlook the essential early steps in quality management. It's just a matter of do the work, check the work, and deliver the work to the client. And that is exactly what happened here.

When TSC got the delivery order, the project engineer got right to work on collecting data. No one did any quality planning or put in place any quality assurance activities. When the engineer completed the writing, he passed it around to a couple other engineers for peer review. This was the quality control step. During peer review, the other engineers made a few comments about word changes or grammar, but nothing substantive about the text. This too, is not unusual. The engineers all work together. They all get along. Nobody is going to do anything that will make someone else look bad in the eyes of the boss because that may come around to the critic on the next project to be peer reviewed. A wise bird does not soil his own nest.

But a project manager that looks only at internal agreement at the expense of customer satisfaction is not all that wise. In this case, the well-intentioned peer review did not serve its intended purpose. It did not offer a critical review of the work product considering customer requirements and expectations. And the organization paid the price for that failure.

Lessons Learned

1. Quality control is only one part of quality management; it is not complete without the others.
2. Quality control can be a make-or-break step in quality management.
3. Quality control actions must be rational, unbiased, and focused on the customer.

Summary

◆ Quality control is a process that monitors and records project results to assess performance and recommend necessary changes.
◆ Quality control is the sixth step in a seven-step quality journey that provides a general framework for quality management.

◆ Quality control results provide feedback to quality assurance; results disclose effectiveness of assurance activities.

◆ In-process inspection plays a key role in quality control. Inspection activities may include measuring, examining, or testing.

◆ Quality control tools are well defined. They are also applied to quality improvement.

◆ Quality improvement is the organized creation of beneficial change.

◆ Quality improvement is the last step in the quality journey.

◆ All quality improvement begins with data collection.

◆ Quality improvement is necessary for many reasons, all associated with customer satisfaction and competitiveness.

◆ Quality improvement is not easy. Hurdles include disillusionment with past efforts, belief that better quality costs more, delegation, and resistance to change.

◆ The plan-do-check-act cycle is a proven model for quality improvement. It includes: *plan* a change that will have beneficial effect, *do* the plan on a small scale, *check* the result to determine effectiveness, *act* to implement the change system-wide if it is effective, or return to the plan step and start over with better information.

Points to Ponder

1. Discuss the role of results in quality control. Why are results important?

2. What is the purpose of inspection in quality control? How may it be best applied?

3. Why is quality improvement necessary? Address this from different points of view.

4. Discuss potential hurdles to quality improvement. How may they be overcome?

5. Describe the plan-do-check-act cycle. Explain the four elements. How is the "check" element related to the subsequently named "study" element?

Exercise

a. Identify a process or activity about which you have personal knowledge. Identify an improvement opportunity. Develop and describe a plan-do-check-act project that will accomplish the improvement. Run the project in real life if you can. If you can't, run a virtual implementation using several imaginary options in the elements.

b. Present your results in class or to a collaborative work group.

References

1. *A Guide to the Project Management Body of Knowledge—Fifth Edition*, Project Management Institute, Newtown Square, PA, 2013, p. 227.
2. Juran, J.M. and De Feo, J.A., Eds., *Juran's Quality Handbook*, 6th ed., McGraw-Hill, New York, 2010, p. 139.

Section III

Tools for Managing Project Quality

7

Collecting and Understanding Project Data

The evolution of quality theory and practice has created a number of tools that may be applied to managing project quality. The tools described in these chapters constitute a set that is generally relevant to project management. Other quality tools may be useful, depending on the project situation. Tools described here fall into five categories, including tools for:

◆ Collecting data
◆ Understanding data
◆ Understanding processes
◆ Analyzing processes
◆ Solving problems

The set includes the seven basic tools of quality described by Ishikawa in his book *Guide to Quality Control*.

◆ Check sheet
◆ Graph
◆ Histogram
◆ Pareto chart
◆ Scatter diagram
◆ Control chart
◆ Cause and effect diagram

Seven additional tools are:

◆ Flow chart
◆ Run chart
◆ Brainstorming
◆ Affinity diagram
◆ Nominal group technique and multivoting
◆ Force field analysis
◆ Pillar diagram

The set also includes two tools, compliance matrix and peer review, that are related to general management, but are so common in use and so relevant to project quality management that any discussion would be incomplete without them.

Tools for Collecting Data

Improper or incomplete collection of data is a fundamental error with an effect that may be magnified many times by subsequent action. Data may be collected in an ad hoc fashion by a quick scan, word of mouth, or even assumption. All of these methods yield unsatisfactory results. A more deliberate method is necessary.

Check Sheet

A check sheet is a simple yet powerful tool for collecting data. It is used to compile and record data from contemporaneous observations or historical data, nothing more. Using a check sheet involves four steps:

1. **Define** events and data. It is important to describe precisely what will be collected and to establish the boundaries of the collection effort. Failure to do this early and well may result in collecting the wrong data, not enough data, or irrelevant data.
2. **Decide** who, what, when, where, how, and why. These aspects of the collection effort are essential to its ultimate success. Determining who collects the data establishes responsibility. What data will be collected is determined by adding detail to the definition of events and data in the previous step to prescribe exact data elements. The

when and where aspects determine the conditions under which the data will be collected. The how aspect describes the collection method and specific instructions for use of the check sheet. Last, it is important to establish the reason for collecting the data (the why aspect) so that data collectors may understand the goal and may then respond appropriately to unexpected situations.

3. **Design** the check sheet. The check sheet should be clear and easy to use. Instructions and terms should be unambiguous. Physical layout should facilitate easy navigation by users and should follow the logical order of the collection sequence of actions.

4. **Collect** data. When all preparations are complete, take action to collect the data.

Although a check sheet is used only to compile and record data, the collected data may provide a foundation for subsequent analysis. Data do not speak for themselves. Users of a check sheet may apply additional analytic skills or tools, or just plain common sense, to obtain meaning from the data collected. Consider the following situation in which a task manager (TM) has just received a "see me" e-mail from the project manager (PM).

TM: Bob, I got your note. What's up?

PM: Have a seat, Jim. You need to do something for me. I was over at the client site yesterday meeting some people and Carol, the client's contract manager, was in the group. She didn't say anything directly to me, but I got the impression she was unhappy with us. Now, she usually works with our contracting office, so I don't have much contact with her. But if something is amiss, I want to know about it before it gets to the program manager and I get a nasty phone call. I don't know what her problem could be. We have the best technical people in the industry working on the project and we're giving them great results. But maybe the engineers are covering something up. Look into it and get back to me.

TM: I'll get right on it.

(Several days go by.)

TM: Bob, got a minute? I've got some information about Carol's concerns.

PM: Sure, what's the deal?

TM: Well, you were right about the technicals. Carol and everybody else over there are really pleased with what we're doing on the technical side. It's the administration that's all messed up.

PM: Administration? That's nonsense. That stuff takes care of itself. Besides, nobody really cares about paperwork; they all want the technical work done right.

TM: Well, it's not nonsense to Carol ...

PM: Look, I've been doing this for thirty-two years. I know what I'm talking about. It's obviously not the administration. You're wasting my time and yours. Haven't you ever heard the axiom "Do not subject to analysis those things that can be solved by inspection?"

TM: Yes, I have. In fact, I worked for the guy who said that some years ago. But I also know the quality axiom "All quality improvement begins with data collection."

PM: Look, don't try to make a big deal out of this. You need to ...

TM: Bob, I know what I "need to" do and I've already done it. I've made up a check sheet and collected some historical data that is very revealing.

PM: Check sheet?

TM: Yes, a check sheet. Let me show you. I went through our contract manager and got an appointment with Carol. I sat down with her and asked about her satisfaction with our overall performance. She is very pleased with our technical work, but is really dissatisfied with our administration. She did not have any details, but said all I had to do was review our monthly status reports and the matter would become clear. When I started looking, I found that almost every monthly status report is returned for correction of some error. Almost every one! No wonder she's not pleased. A really in-depth analysis would involve a lot of people and take a lot of time. I knew you wanted a quick answer, so I just did it myself. I made up a little check sheet—that's a tool for compiling and recording data in an organized way—and pulled the status report files for the last six months. I went through the first month to identify possible sources of error and set up a check sheet with the sources all listed so I could just make a tick mark in the appropriate row when I encountered that particular error. I then summarized the data in a column over on the right. Here's the result.

(Shows him the check sheet in Figure 7.1.)

Monthly Status Report Error Check Sheet	
Period Covered: January – June	
Error Description	Number
Technical Error Summary	0
Administrative Error Summary	100
Late submission: ///	3
Date error: /	1
Period covered error: /	1
Charge code number error: ///// ///// ///// ///// ///// ///// ///// ///// ///// //	47
Hours billed error: ///// ///// ///// ///// ///// ///// ///	33
Materials charge error: ////	4
Travel charge error: /////	5
Other direct cost error: ///	3
Attachments error: //	2
Number of copies error: /	1

Figure 7.1. Monthly status report error check sheet.

TM: The data show not one single error related to technical matters over the past six months. No content errors in reports, no miscalculations, no wrong methods applied. Nothing. But administration is another story. Ten different errors occurred during the period examined.

PM: Well, I can fix that. There's no excuse for late reports or missing attachments. I'll just make it clear that this is unacceptable and apply disciplinary action if necessary to get things right.

TM: Bob, we should keep in mind that these are just numbers. A check sheet does not tell us any more than that. If we want to fix things, we'll have to determine why errors occur. And we can't do everything at once. We should start with the things that will have the greatest improvement effect.

PM: Which ones are those?

TM: Well, that's another kind of analysis. Let me get back to you on that.

PM: OK, but don't take too long. I don't want this to bite me.

In this situation, the task manager made effective use of the check sheet to compile and record data relevant to a matter of concern. The project manager seemed unsure about the source of the concern and predisposed to a likely cause. The task manager used the check sheet to collect data that disclosed the true nature of the problem and provided a foundation for subsequent analysis and action.

One final point on nomenclature: A check *sheet* is used to collect data; a check*list* (an entirely different tool) is used to establish things to do. The task manager used a check sheet to identify errors. He might now prepare a checklist of things to do in order to prepare monthly status reports to ensure correctness.

Tools for Understanding Data

Four tools may be helpful to project managers to understand data: graphs, histograms, Pareto charts, and scatter diagrams.

Graphs

Graphs are one of Ishikawa's seven basic tools. The purpose of a graph is to organize, summarize, and display data, usually over time. Ishikawa described three different types of graphs, including line graphs, bar graphs, and circle graphs. Four steps are involved in preparing graphs:

1. **Define** events and data. As with the check sheet, it is important to determine what information will be addressed in the graph.
2. **Design** the graph. Select the type of graph to be used, considering the data and the audience of the graph.
3. **Collect** data if this has not already been done. A check sheet may be useful for this step. Data may be collected incrementally and cumulatively over time.
4. **Enter** data. Prepare the graph by entering data.

The line graph is a form commonly used to report project financial information. The "burn" chart may be familiar to many with project management experience. It shows how available funds are being "burned up" (that is, expended) during project implementation (see Figure 7.2). This line graph shows how project expenditures are progressing over time in relation to the project budget. It shows that expenditures are currently $80,000 below budget.

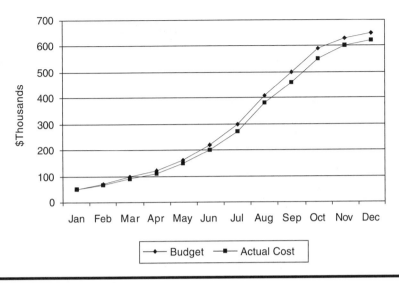

Figure 7.2. A "Burn" chart.

A bar graph displays data as vertical or horizontal bars. It can show data over time or data at a single point in time. Figure 7.3 shows a bar graph that displays project budget and expense data by quarter for a twelve-month period.

A circle graph (often called a "pie chart") is useful for displaying data when the relationships between data elements and the whole are more important than showing data over time. Figure 7.4 shows a circle graph that displays the composition of a project team by level of education.

Histograms

A histogram is a type of bar graph that deals with data that exist in a continuous range from a low number to a high number. Histograms display frequency distribution, or how often (frequency) individual data points occur across the range of the data from low to high (distribution). Histograms summarize data in a form that is more easily understood than a table of collected numbers. Creating and using a histogram requires six steps:

1. **Select** the measures to be examined. Typical measures are things like size, speed, time, weight, dimensions, and so on.

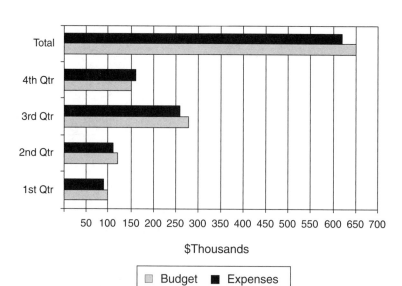

Figure 7.3.   Project budget and expense data.

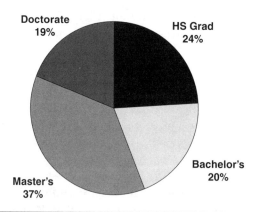

Figure 7.4.   Project team education levels.

2. **Collect** the data. Again, a check sheet may be useful. Data may already exist in some sort of spreadsheet or tabular form.
3. **Prepare** a frequency table. This is the first step in organizing the data. It is a summary of data in a sequential format.

4. **Design** the histogram. Histograms are constructed in a disciplined way. Throwing the data together in a way that seems convenient at the moment may result in a display that is completely useless.
5. **Draw** the histogram. Enter the data and prepare the graphic display. Most word-processing and spreadsheet programs include chart-making capabilities that will be helpful in this step.
6. **Interpret** the data. View the bars of the histogram and analyze their relationship to each other.

As an example, consider the task manager who just received an additional assignment from the project manager to look into contract processing time. The project manager has a feeling that processing time is too long and wants some data to either confirm or dispel his concerns. The task manager prepares a check sheet and starts collecting data on the number of days required to process individual contracts during the past year. He collects a lot of data because every purchase associated with the project is a contract, even routine purchases of office supplies. He then arranges the data sequentially in a frequency table that shows the number of days required for processing and the number of contracts. The frequency distribution is shown in Figure 7.5.

The collected data show that contract processing time ranged from sixteen to sixty-five days during the period examined. A total of twenty-five contracts were awarded during this time. To enhance clarity in this example, data have been shown in five columns. If the data were shown in one or two columns, it would be difficult to make any sense of them. That is where a histogram comes in.

Contract Processing Time									
days	contracts	days	contracts	days	contracts	days	contracts	days	contracts
16	1	26	0	36	1	46	0	56	0
17	0	27	0	37	0	47	0	57	0
18	0	28	1	38	2	48	2	58	1
19	0	29	0	39	0	49	0	59	0
20	1	30	1	40	4	50	0	60	0
21	0	31	0	41	0	51	1	61	0
22	0	32	2	42	2	52	0	62	0
23	0	33	0	43	0	53	0	63	0
24	1	34	1	44	0	54	3	64	0
25	0	35	0	45	0	55	0	65	1

Figure 7.5. Frequency distribution for contract processing time.

The first step in designing a histogram is to select the number of bars to appear on the chart. This is called the class interval. The histogram will not display each number of processing days as a separate bar. Instead, numbers of days will be grouped together into classes. This can be a little tricky. If too many classes are used, the bars tend to be rather low and of similar height, making analysis difficult. If too few classes are used, bars tend to be rather high and of similar height, again making analysis difficult. An appropriate number of classes is determined by taking the square root of the number of observations or data points. The data include twenty-five contracts (the number of observations), so the appropriate number of classes is the square root of twenty-five, or five.

The next step in designing a histogram is to determine the range of values to be included in each class or bar. This is called the class width. This is determined by dividing the range of data values by the class interval. The lowest observation is sixteen and the highest is sixty-five. The range between sixteen and sixty-five inclusive of both ends is fifty, so the class width is equal to fifty divided by five, or ten. Each bar on the histogram will include ten processing days. The resulting histogram, when drawn, is shown in Figure 7.6.

This form of display makes interpretation a bit easier. The task manager can tell at a glance that processing time seems to form a normal distribution; it seems to follow a bell-shaped curve. The most frequent processing time for

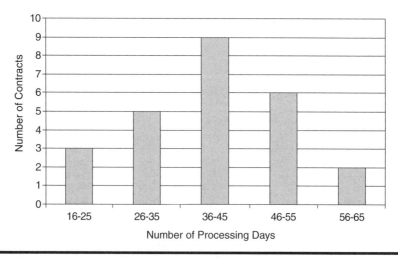

Figure 7.6.   Contract processing time histogram.

contracts awarded during the period studied was thirty-six to forty-five days. Fewer contracts, and about the same number each, required twenty-six to thirty-five or forty-six to fifty-five days. And still fewer, and again about the same number each, required sixteen to twenty-five or fifty-six to sixty-five days. From these data, the task manager could probably determine an average processing time that might be useful for planning. The data might also suggest something about the nature of contracts or the award process. The data shown may suggest that an average processing time would be relevant for planning purposes. If the data showed large numbers of contracts at the low end and large numbers at the high end, the task manager might not consider an average time to be useful. Rather, he might do further analysis to determine why some contracts are processed quickly and some require a much longer time. Additional analysis will require additional tools.

Pareto Charts

A Pareto chart is a helpful tool to identify the greatest opportunity for improvement among a number of possibilities and to identify the small number of most influential causes (the "vital few") among the complete set of possible sources of error. It is named for Vilfredo Pareto, an Italian economist, who determined through study that wealth seems to be distributed in populations according to an 80/20 rule: 80 percent of the wealth is controlled by 20 percent of the population. This rule also seems to be valid for defects in administrative and production processes: 80 percent of the defects are caused by 20 percent of the possible sources of error.

A Pareto chart is a bar graph with data in descending order. This deliberate arrangement of data in descending order from left to right on the chart is its signature characteristic. So the first step in preparing a Pareto chart is to create a bar graph with the defect or error data arranged in descending order. The left-hand scale (the y-axis of the chart) should account for the total number of defects (see Figure 7.7).

The next step is to add a cumulative percentage scale on the right-hand side of the chart. This is a second scale along the vertical or y-axis that mirrors the scale along the left-hand side. The cumulative percentage curve is a line graph that extends over the top of the bar data. The curve is plotted as a series of connected points that are obtained by successively adding the values of data from left to right and dividing by the total. For example, the first point along the cumulative percentage curve is determined by dividing the value of

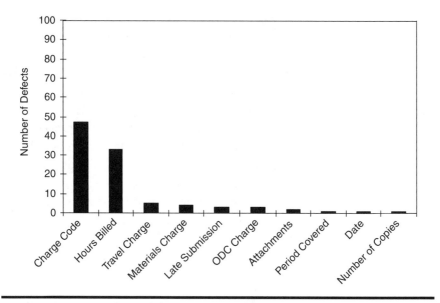

Figure 7.7. Pareto chart, defect/error data only.

the first data bar on the left by the total number of defects or errors. The second point is determined by adding the first two data bars and then dividing by the total. Then add the first three and divide by the total and so on until all points have been determined and plotted on the chart. The result is shown in Figure 7.8.

Pareto charts disclose two important bits of information. First, the left-most bar indicates the greatest opportunity for improvement because it represents the source of error responsible for the most defects. Second, the Pareto chart identifies the "vital few," those few sources of error that account for most of the defects or errors. To define the vital few, go up the right-hand scale to the 80 percent point. Then move to the left across the chart until you meet the cumulative percentage curve. Drop straight down to the horizontal axis. All the sources of error to the left of this point are those that account for 80 percent of the defects or errors. Eliminate these few, these vital few, sources of error and 80 percent of the defects in the process go with them. Recall the task manager and his assignment to improve the contracting situation.

TM: Bob, got a minute?
PM: Sure, what's up.

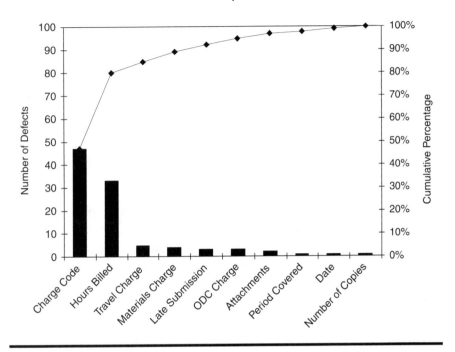

Figure 7.8.   Pareto chart.

TM: When we spoke the other day about contracting, I said I would get back to you about what we should do first. So I'd like to show you a Pareto chart.

PM: A what?

TM: A Pareto chart. Kind of an unusual name I guess. It's named for an Italian economist who did some studies about the distribution of wealth in populations. He found that there is an 80/20 relationship between wealth and people that seems to hold true for administrative and production processes, too.

PM: What do you mean?

TM: Any process may include a number of sources of defects. But the errors in the process are not equally distributed across all sources. A couple of the sources seem to account for most of the problems. It's about an 80/20 ratio; 80 percent of the problems come from 20 percent of the sources. And by the way, don't we see that among team members, too? In a large team, it seems that a couple of people are the real workhorses ...

PM: Like you, for instance?

TM: Well ... and a couple of people seem to be the problem children who take up a lot of management time.

PM: Boy howdy!

TM: A Pareto chart is a specialized tool that helps identify that small number of sources that cause most of the problems. They're called the "vital few."

PM: How does it do that?

TM: Look at this.

(Shows him the chart.)

TM: A Pareto chart starts with a bar graph that has the bars deliberately arranged in descending order from left to right. The bar farthest to the left represents the highest numbers of defects, so it is the area of greatest opportunity for improvement—the area we should fix first.

PM: Well, that seems pretty obvious. I don't need a Pareto chart to tell me that.

TM: You're right. These data are pretty straightforward. But not all data are. In a more complex situation, we could have twenty-five or thirty potential sources of error with several being relatively equal. And another thing ... do you recall what you said when I first showed you the check sheet with the ten sources?

PM: Yes. I thought I'd fix the late reports and missing attachments first.

TM: Right. If we did that, we'd spend money and time eliminating 5 percent of the errors. People can tend to go after sources that seem easiest to fix or are in some way attractive to them. A Pareto chart forces us to consider the data and go after the things that have the most effect on the process.

PM: But it's more than just the first bar, right?

TM: Exactly. And that's where the other unique feature of a Pareto chart comes into play. Look at this percentage scale over on the right side of the chart. You don't see that elsewhere. It mirrors the defect scale on the left side. The 100 percent mark equals the total number of defects on the left. And look at this line across the top.

PM: Yeah, I've been wondering what that was.

TM: It's called a cumulative percentage curve. It's plotted by taking the percent of the total that each bar plus every bar to its left represents. So it's cumulative moving to the right. See?

PM: Got it.

TM: What we do is, we go to the 80 percent point on the right-hand scale, then move straight across to the left until we intersect with the cumulative percentage curve. We drop straight down and there we have it. We have just defined the vital few. The bars to the left of this point account for 80 percent of the defects. If we fix these two sources of error, we'll eliminate 80 percent of the problem, not 5 percent.

PM: And Carol is a lot happier with our administration.

TM: Right!

PM: You know, this looks complex, but it's really pretty simple.

TM: It sure is. Once you understand it, a Pareto chart is a powerful tool that is easy to use. And our standard office software has a utility for making these charts, so they are readily accessible.

PM: That's good work, Jim. Let's get on it.

TM: Already started. Now that we understand the data, we'll have to do some analysis before we take action. We want effective actions, not trial and error. And as you might have guessed, that's another chart.

One last point about Pareto charts is important to understand. Pareto charts usually deal with the number of defects, and subsequent action is intended to reduce the number. Sometimes the number of defects or errors is not as important as the cost or the effect of the error. Consider accidents at an oil-drilling field site. Accidents have a cost in lost time, medical claims, and human suffering. Suppose research showed that for every 100,000 labor hours, there are seven accidents involving workers who slip and fall on wet, slick soil. The resulting cost is a bump or bruise, a couple of pain pills, and perhaps some liniment. Suppose the data also show that for every 100,000 labor hours, there is one accident in which a worker gets a hand caught in steel cables and suffers a traumatic amputation of one or more fingers. The resulting cost is much more lost time, perhaps a temporary suspension of work, and a great deal of human suffering. The goal should be to eliminate the one accident, not the seven. When cost of errors is more significant than number of errors, simply construct the Pareto chart in a way that expresses the cost of the errors, not the number.

Scatter Diagrams

A scatter diagram identifies possible relationships between two variables. Understanding relationships among data elements is essential to understanding the data as a whole. The steps in creating a scatter diagram include:

1. **Define** the theoretical relationship. Relationships between variables are not always obvious. Relationships are also easy to assume. This first step identifies the two variables that will be formally examined.
2. **Collect** 50 to 100 paired samples of data. Analysis must be based on a sufficient amount of data. Too few data may result in erroneous conclusions that arise from random flukes among the limited data.
3. **Plot** the data on x-y axes. The x-axis, the horizontal axis, should be used for the independent variable; that is, the variable that is the base. The data of the other variable will change in some regular way as the base changes if there is a relationship between the two. The y-axis should be used for the dependent variable; that is, the variable that may change in some regular way as the base changes.
4. **Interpret** the data. Look for regular patterns among the plotted points.

Recall the task manager who was looking into contract processing time. Using a histogram, he determined that contract processing time varied from sixteen to sixty-five days, but why did some contracts require more time than others? The task manager suspects that some kind of relationship exists between the variables that influence the contracting process. Perhaps processing time is related to the dollar value of the contract. Perhaps it is related to the time of year during which the contract is processed.

A scatter diagram identifies possible relationships between variables. The task manager can use a scatter diagram to investigate relationships, two at a time. He collects a little more data so he has at least fifty data points. Some of the data points are the same (that is, some contracts required the same amount of time to process), so the chart will not necessarily show fifty separate data points. He then plots the data on a scatter diagram with the dollar value on the x-axis and the processing time on the y-axis. This is because he believes that processing time (a dependent variable) may change in some regular way as the dollar value (the independent variable) changes. The result is shown in Figure 7.9.

Notice that the data for each level of contract value are close together. The task manager could almost draw a single line from left to right connecting all

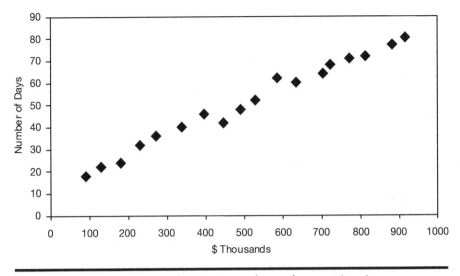

Figure 7.9. Scatter diagram for contract value and processing time.

the data points. Data grouped together like this suggest a strong relationship between contract value and processing time. As the contract value increases, the processing time also increases in a somewhat uniform way.

The task manager may also suspect that processing time is related in some way to the time of year during which the contract is processed. Perhaps contracts take more time to process during traditional vacation periods when staffing levels might be reduced. So he collects the time-of-year data for the contracts he is analyzing and prepares a scatter diagram with the month on the x-axis and the processing time on the y-axis. This result is shown in Figure 7.10.

Now the data points are all over the diagram. There does not seem to be any grouping of data for each month or any kind of regular pattern at all. This kind of grouping (or lack of grouping) suggests that no relationship exists between contract processing time and the time of year that the contract is processed. The rule of interpretation is simple: The closer the grouping (the more the data approximate a line), the stronger the relationship; the wider the grouping (the more the data are randomly scattered about the diagram), the weaker the relationship.

The task manager must remember another rule of interpretation: Scatter diagrams are not predictive. They only disclose the relationship between data elements based on data that have been collected. They do not predict future

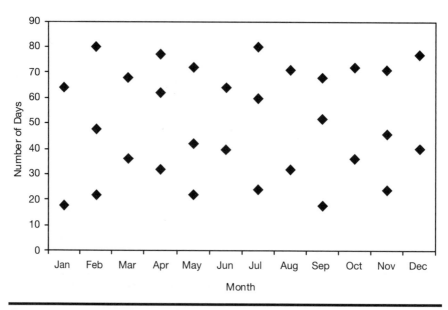

Figure 7.10.   Scatter diagram for time of year and processing time.

relationships that go beyond the collected data. Consider a scatter diagram that addresses the relationship between human age and height. Age is on the x-axis and height is on the y-axis. Data have been collected from a sample of 100 people with ages ranging from one year to eighteen years. The data show a strong relationship between age and height. As people advance in age, they grow taller. The diagram shows a height of about six feet when the data stop at age eighteen. Based on collected data, a projected height at age thirty-six might be twelve feet. This, of course, is nonsense. But for data less familiar, it might be a reasonable prediction—except for the fact that scatter diagrams are not predictive. Users must restrict interpretation and their subsequent conclusions to only the data at hand.

In the contracting example, the task manager cannot predict that contracts with values over $1 million will require more than sixty-five days to process. It may be that $1 million is a threshold in the contracting office. Below that amount, one contract manager handles the processing. As contract value goes up and contracts become more complex, more time is required for processing by a single individual. But over $1 million, contracts are assigned to a team of contract specialists who work simultaneously. Data collected above the $1 million value point would show a dramatic decrease in processing time due to the additional resources applied.

Summary

◆ Quality tools provide a mechanism for managing project quality.

◆ A check sheet may be used to compile and record data from contemporaneous observations or historical records. A check *sheet* includes a collection of data. A check*list* describes things to do.

◆ Graphs may be used to organize, summarize, and display data over time. A line graph shows how data change over time. A bar graph shows how data change and how separate data elements are related to each other. A pie graph shows how data elements are related to each other, especially how separate elements constitute a whole.

◆ A histogram is used to summarize data and to show a frequency distribution; that is, how data elements are distributed across a range of values. Class interval (the number of bars on the histogram) is determined by the square root of the total number of data points. Class width (the data range within each bar) is determined by the total data range divided by the class interval.

◆ A Pareto chart is a bar graph with bars arranged in descending order from left to right. The bars represent sources of error, and the values of the bars reflect the number of defects. The left-most bar (the category with the greatest number of data points) represents the greatest opportunity for improvement. A Pareto chart includes a cumulative percentage curve that helps identify the "vital few," the small number of sources of error (about 20 percent) that account for most of the defects (about 80 percent).

◆ When the cost of defects is more important than the number of defects, a Pareto chart should be constructed so that bars represent the cost of defects rather than the number.

◆ Scatter diagrams identify possible relationships between two variables. Close groupings of data points suggest a strong relationship. Very wide groupings or widely dispersed data points suggest weak relationships or no relationship. Scatter diagrams cannot be used to predict values outside the range of data included in the diagram.

Points to Ponder

1. Describe the four steps in developing a check sheet for collecting data. Why is a check sheet useful? How is it different from a checklist?

2. Explain how line graphs, bar graphs, and circle graphs might be used for understanding different types of data. Why not use the same type of graph for all types of data?
3. Why is a histogram a special type of bar graph? Describe how data are organized and how the graph is constructed.
4. Explain why a Pareto chart is a special type of bar graph. Describe how the data are arranged and how the data are interpreted.
5. What is the purpose of a scatter diagram? Describe how it is constructed and how the data are interpreted. Can scatter diagrams be used to look to the future?

Exercises

1. Create a check sheet for collecting data about something that interests you. Be creative, e.g., go to a fast food restaurant during lunch and collect data on orders for a given period. (You may need the manager's permission to do this.)
2. Prepare a line graph, bar graph, and circle graph using simple data that are available to you.
3. Prepare a histogram with data that are readily available to you, e.g., the individual height of your classmates and all their family members.
4. Prepare a Pareto chart with data that are available to you. If you visit a fast food restaurant for Exercise 1, perhaps you could use the individual menu items as categories. They are not defects *per se*, but may provide the data necessary to construct and interpret the chart.
5. Prepare a scatter diagram using data available to you. If you collected height data in Exercise 3, perhaps you could link this with age data and use that for one axis, height for the other.

8

Understanding Project Processes

Understanding data is important, but it is only an early step in managing project quality. Data are the voices of processes. When performed, processes produce some kind of result. Data are the expressions of those results. The next step in managing project quality is to understand processes.

Tools for Understanding Processes

Three quality tools for understanding processes are useful for project managers. One of them is probably familiar to most project managers. The other two may be less familiar because of their traditional application to manufacturing processes.

Flow Charts

Flow charts are probably familiar to most project managers. They are common tools of basic management. A flow chart identifies the sequence of events in a process. Beyond that, it allows—even forces—identification of the sometimes-obscure elements in a process. Using flow charts requires six deliberate actions:

1. **Set** boundaries. A common problem among novices or the overly enthusiastic is that they try to flow-chart the world. This approach

seldom has a happy result. The individual or team should decide what they will consider in the flow-charting effort and what they will exclude. A good result often depends on properly framing the effort at the start. The team should also agree on the level of detail to be obtained. A top-level macro view may be all that is necessary at the moment.

2. **Determine** the steps in the process. Before attempting to draw the chart, identify the basic framework of inputs, outputs, activities, and decisions.

3. **Establish** the sequence of process steps. This can be done effectively with a lot of "sticky notes" and wall space. Involve the team so that different views may be considered. It is important, and sometimes difficult, to describe the sequence as it is, not as it should be. Performance results arise from what *is* occurring, not what is expected to occur.

4. **Draw** the flow chart. Automated tools are available to do this. These tools may include a variety of symbols to represent elements in the chart. The five basic symbols shown in Figure 8.1 may be sufficient for most project flow charts. Keep things simple. Add the level of detail necessary to understand the process. Trying to include the lowest possible level of detail may only result in a morass of symbols and lines that is unintelligible and of little value. Use simple words to describe activities and be consistent in both construction and language.

5. **Test** the flow chart for completeness and accuracy. First, ensure that the chart is constructed correctly and that all symbols are properly used. Review the process flow to ensure that all activities are included and fully addressed. Beware of "magic happens" activities, those that suggest some kind of activity or result but do not include all the essential elements. It may be helpful to obtain a review by someone not directly involved in the effort, but who is knowledgeable about the process. Such a person may help overcome blind spots or identify process steps not readily apparent to those analyzing the process and preparing the chart. Above all, ensure that the chart reflects the way the process *really* works, not the way it should work.

6. **Finalize** the chart. Put the chart in final form using consistent fonts and graphic alignment. A well-organized chart, even a "pretty" chart, is easier to read and understand.

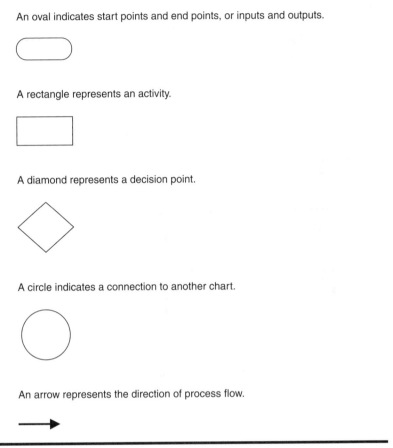

An oval indicates start points and end points, or inputs and outputs.

A rectangle represents an activity.

A diamond represents a decision point.

A circle indicates a connection to another chart.

An arrow represents the direction of process flow.

Figure 8.1. Flow chart basic symbols.

Recall the task manager who used a check sheet to compile and record errors and then used a Pareto chart to identify the vital few sources of error in the process. He may now use a flow chart to identify the sequence of events in the process of preparing monthly status reports and, in so doing, identify where and how things might go wrong. The flow chart in Figure 8.2 shows the report preparation process.

The task manager carefully considers the final flow chart and determines if the process, as shown, may be reasonably expected to produce correct reports if all goes well. He then refers to his initial check sheet and compares the sources of error to the flow chart to determine how errors might occur.

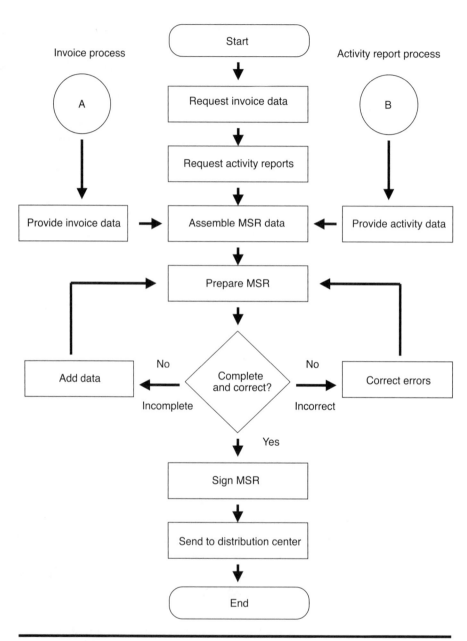

Figure 8.2.   Monthly status report preparation process flow chart.

For example, late submission could be a result of delays in any of the steps shown on the flow chart, but if all goes well during the preparation process, late submission probably results from some kind of delay in the distribution center after the task manager hands off the report. Errors in the date of the report or the period covered probably occur during the "prepare MSR" step because that is where this information is added to the report.

The two most significant sources of error, charge code number errors and hours-billed errors, may occur outside the process addressed by this flow chart. The task manager determines that these data are entered into the monthly status report "as is" from the invoice data provided by the accounting office. Whatever errors are present must be occurring in the accounting office or in the reporting process that provides the data to accounting. Further analysis and probably another flow chart are required.

Run Charts

A run chart is used to observe process performance over time. It is a line graph with data that *vary around a centerline*, usually the mean. It is used for repeatable processes where performance is expected to be stable. A run chart will show defect trends, shifts, or cycles. To create a run chart:

1. **Identify** the process to be observed. Make sure the process involves some kind of repeatable activity in which results are expected to be consistent over time. A run chart has no value in areas where data are expected to change, as in a chart showing profits (expected to go up over time) or customer complaints (expected to go down over time).

2. **Collect** data. Usually twenty to twenty-five data points are required for a meaningful chart.

3. **Create** the graph. As stated, a run chart is a line graph with data that vary about a centerline. Plot the data on an x-y axis graph, then calculate and plot the mean. Do not recalculate the mean when you add new data. Only recalculate the mean after you change the process. Initial data collection establishes the process mean. Subsequent data must be evaluated against that mean unless the process has been changed since initial data collection.

4. **Interpret** the data. Look for trends, shifts in data groupings, or cycles. All may suggest further analysis to determine the reason.

As an example, consider commute time, or the time required for project team members to travel from their homes to the office. The task manager has noticed that tardiness has been an occasional problem, but has some regular aspects. When one person is late, many seem to be late, and it seems that some days of the week have a higher incidence of tardiness than others. He would like to see people at work on time and is tempted to issue a directive with a threat of punishment for late arrivers, but he thinks there may be factors beyond employees' control that are affecting arrival times. He collects data from all employees for a twenty-day period. He computes daily averages and plots the data on a run chart (see Figure 8.3).

The run chart shows a repeatable process: People commute to work every day. It also shows a process that is expected to be rather stable: Travel time may vary according to traffic and weather, but generally the commute time should be about the same every day. The first thing that the task manager notices is that there are two "spikes," examples of extreme deviation from the mean. He recalls that a truck overturned recently and closed the main highway for several hours during morning rush hour. The run chart shows an average of 120 minutes for the commute on that day. A few weeks later, a federal holiday occurred on a Monday. Many businesses were closed, but not the project office. Team members experienced a significantly shorter commute due to reduced traffic.

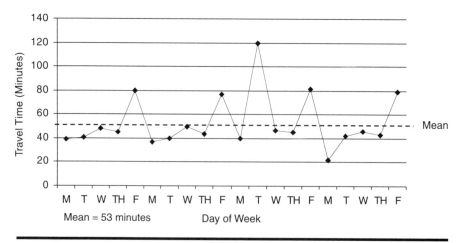

Figure 8.3.   Run chart for commute time.

After a little more study, the task manager notices a regular pattern of data points significantly above the mean. These points occur every Friday. Seems reasonable, he thinks. Traffic always seems to be heavier on Friday. He is about to send an e-mail to all team members advising them to get an earlier start on Fridays so they can arrive at the office on time when Amy stops by his work cube.

> Amy: Jim, got a minute?
>
> TM: Sure, what can I do for you?
>
> Amy: Well, remember last week when you asked Larry to collect data from all of us about our morning commute time? I asked Larry to give me a copy and I've prepared what's called a run chart. It shows how data vary over time, but more important, how data vary around a centerline, usually the mean. Take a look at this chart. Other than the two exceptions, the day there was an accident and the day of the federal holiday, it shows that Friday is consistently a bad commute day. And we see that in the office. A lot of people are late on Fridays, and everybody is generally out of sorts because of the bad commute.
>
> TM: Yeah, I know. I made a similar chart and I was just about to send out a note telling people to get an earlier start on Fridays.
>
> Amy: Jim, that's going to be a lead balloon. I've got a better idea. Why don't we adopt a flex-time schedule where people can work extra hours during the week and take a Friday off every pay period? Or better yet, why don't we do telecommuting and allow people to work from home on Fridays? We'll contribute to reducing traffic, save fuel consumption, and make people a lot happier—and I'll bet a lot more productive—on Fridays. What do you think?

The task manager thought Amy had a pretty good idea. It was an idea that made sense to him because of the data, and it was an idea that he could propose and defend to the project manager because it was based on data, not intuition or personal choice.

The matter of contract processing time provides another example, perhaps one more closely related to project actions. Previously, the task manager used a histogram to understand the data, to see how processing time was distributed across the range of values. Now he uses a run chart to see how processing time varies around the mean. He collects data for a twelve-week period. For each week, he calculates the average processing time for all contracts that were processed to completion during the week. He plots the data on a run chart as shown in Figure 8.4.

The task manager has just heard from the project manager that the program manager told him that the vice president for operations wants all contracts processed and awarded by the end of August so that the contracting office can use September to put everything in order in preparation for the new fiscal year that begins on October 1st. He wonders if these people ever make decisions based on data or ever consider the effect that their directives have on the work force. He knows that September is always extremely unpleasant for his friends in contracting because of all the extra hours required to meet this annual management directive. And he knows that he and other task managers make the situation worse by dumping as many contract actions as possible on the contracting office late in the year knowing none will be processed during September and will have to be completed by the end of August.

Looking for a better way, he begins to analyze the run chart. Because the average processing time is forty-two days, his first thought is that the contracting office should stop accepting new contract actions forty-two working days before the end of August. That means around the first of July, but that is only the average. Contracts requiring more than forty-two days to process would still create extra hours of work in order to be completed unless an equal number requiring less than forty-two days were in the queue. Maybe

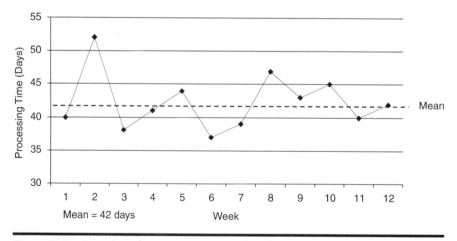

Figure 8.4. Run chart for contract processing time.

the cutoff date should be fifty-two working days before the end of August, an amount of time equal to the highest number of days shown by the current data. This does not seem like a good solution. Besides, the contracting office is unlikely to announce that it will stop serving customers on the first of July or before.

The task manager takes another look at the scatter diagram prepared earlier to determine that contract processing time seems to be related in some way to the dollar value of the contract. After a little thought, he decides that the best solution is one that involves all the participants, not one that just dumps the problem onto the contracting office. He develops a progressive schedule of lead times for distribution to task managers. Lead times are based on expected processing times related to contract value. This schedule will advise task managers that if they anticipate a contract action of a certain amount, they should have the action to the contract office by a certain number of days before August 31st. Now, task managers will have information they can use for planning, the contracting office will probably receive contract actions within more reasonable time frames, and the contracting office can extend receipt of low-dollar-value contracts into September because of assured available processing time. All of this is possible because the task manager applied quality tools to understand data and processes: a histogram, a scatter diagram, and a run chart. Sometimes the centerline is not a mean, but a zero value. For example, a project manager may want to observe how expenditures are progressing during project implementation. The goal is to spend all the available money, but no more. A run chart might be constructed that shows a centerline of zero, which represents the authorized budget, with data plotted as percentages above and below the authorized budget. In this kind of chart, the actual budget amounts are not important and not shown. Only the percentages above and below the currently authorized budget amount are displayed.

Control Charts

Control charts are very powerful tools for monitoring, controlling, and improving processes over time. They are one of the most complex quality tools and probably the most little used outside of manufacturing domains. Control charts are applicable to administrative processes. Data speak, sometimes loudly and sometimes more subtly. Control charts, as "the voice of the process," can speak volumes of useful information. Like run charts, control charts are useful to analyze repeatable processes in which results are expected to be stable over time. It is a mistake to attempt to apply control charts to processes in which results may change over time. Control charts:

♦ Disclose the nature of variation in the process
♦ Indicate what should be expected
♦ Indicate what lies outside of expectations

Control charts use sample data to generalize about a population. Small amounts of data, properly selected—and that usually means randomly selected—can provide sufficient information to make process decisions. Control charts use two types of data: attribute and variable. Attribute data are binary. Something is or is not. Something is go or no-go. A report is either late or not late; the degree of lateness is irrelevant. Variable data are some kind of measurement. An environmental project may be concerned not about the presence or absence of contaminants in groundwater but about the level of contamination as measured on a continuous scale of parts per million. Control charts are the basic tools of statistical process control, which has been and continues to be widely used in manufacturing. The traditional manner of application may be a hindrance to their use in project settings. Project managers may assume that control charts are restricted to manufacturing and not relevant to processes more administrative in nature. Both production and administration include processes that are repeatable, processes in which results are expected to be stable over time. Control charts are applicable in either domain. Consider the following situation.

Johnson Medical Services (JMS) processes and pays medical claims for insurance providers in a fourteen-state area. Claims are screened for correctness at seventy-two collection centers, corrected by direct contact with the claimant, and then sent to the accounting division for payment. One or more errors of any kind in the claim identified in accounting requires the claim to be returned to the claimant at significant cost to JMS and inconvenience to the claimant.

JMS management is dissatisfied with the current costs of erroneous claims and the level of expressed customer satisfaction with returned claims. JMS has awarded a contract to a management consulting firm to conduct an analysis of the situation and determine how many erroneous claims are slipping through the collection center screening.

The assigned project manager believes that collecting data on all errors from all collection centers will require time and money that far exceeds the available budget. She contacts a statistician who advises her that complete population data are unnecessary; sample data will provide valid information. In coordination with the statistician, she decides to select four collection centers at random, then collect fifty random samples of reviewed claims from each center over a five-day period. Having done that, she prepares a summary chart as shown in Figure 8.5.

Looking at the data generates several questions for the project manager. All four centers did not show the exact same number of errors. Errors varied widely from day to day. Center A had five errors on Friday, but had seventeen errors on Monday. Should performance on Friday be the expectation? Is "zero defects" not the expectation? Should Monday's performance be punished in some way? Center A had a total of forty-one errors for the five days; Center C had sixty.

This may seem confusing. A control chart will help to make things clear. Recall that control charts are tools for monitoring, controlling, and improving processes over time, and recall that control charts may be applied only to repeatable processes. The claim review process is a repeatable process. The same people review the same forms day after day. The steps in the review process are the same even though the details of individual claims may vary from one to another. Results are expected to be stable over time. The same number of errors, preferably no errors at all, should occur over time.

The project manager has all the data she needs to prepare a control chart. The first step is to determine just what kind of chart. Control charts exist in eight basic varieties, all responding to different conditions. The right chart is determined by the type of data being examined and by the sample size. The statistician advises the project manager that, in this case, something called an

	Center A	Center B	Center C	Center D	Total	Average
Monday	17	8	9	10	44	
Tuesday	6	7	9	16	38	
Wednesday	7	10	14	8	39	
Thursday	6	8	16	11	41	
Friday	5	11	12	9	37	
Total	41	44	60	54	199	
Average						9.95

Figure 8.5.   Erroneous medical claim forms.

np chart should be used. An *np* chart deals with the number of defects among attribute data with samples of constant size.

The next step is to plot the data on a graph and also plot the mean (see Figure 8.6). This looks like a run chart because it is. A control chart is a run chart with an added feature: upper and lower control limits. Determining control limits can be a little bit scary. Control limits are calculated differently for each of the eight basic types of charts. The calculation for *np* charts is rather straightforward. The data shown in Figure 8.5 provide some numbers directly. Other numbers are a matter of simple calculation. Figure 8.7 shows the necessary information.

Total number of defects, total number of samples taken, and the average defects per sample (the mean) are taken directly from the chart. Sample size was predetermined. Other numbers are calculated as follows:

Total number of observations = Sample size times
total number of samples taken

Defect proportion of total = Total number of defects divided by
total number of observations

In an *np* chart, control limits are derived according to the following formula:

The mean plus or minus three times the square root of the mean
times one minus the proportion

or

$$\text{Mean} \pm 3 \sqrt{\text{mean}}\,(1 - \text{proportion})$$

The upper control limit is the "mean plus" result and the lower control limit is the "mean minus" result. Performing the calculations yields an upper control limit of eighteen and a lower control limit of one. To complete the control chart, plot the upper and lower control limits on the graph as shown in Figure 8.8.

Once the mechanics of control chart construction have been completed, evaluation of the data can begin. Control charts are described as the "voice of the process" because they indicate how the process is performing. The project manager's question about what kind of results can be expected is answered by the control limits. These values are derived statistically to show the range of normal process performance. As the process is currently performing, any sample of fifty reports may be expected to include one to eighteen defective

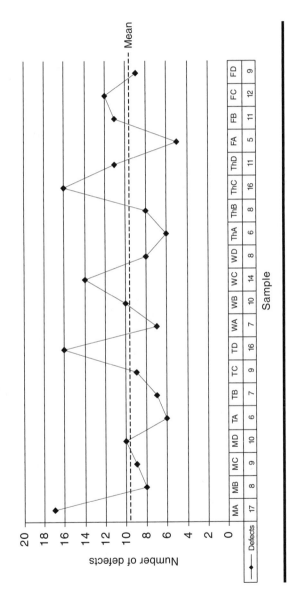

Figure 8.6. Constructing a control chart: first step.

Data Element	Value
Total number of defects	199
Total number of samples taken	20
Average defects per sample (mean)	9.95
Sample size	50
Total number of observations	1000
Defect proportion of total	0.199

Figure 8.7.   Control chart calculation data.

reports. This range of defects will not change in the future unless the process is changed. Any repeatable process includes variation. Results are not precisely the same; results will vary. How much will they vary? The control chart defines the upper and lower extremes. It tells managers what they may reasonably expect from the process.

Two types of variation affect process performance: random cause and special cause. Random cause variation, sometimes called common cause variation, is inherent in the system. It is always present. It cannot be specifically identified. An example might be a low level of illumination in the work area. This may make it difficult for medical claim form processors to read the forms accurately, resulting in occasional errors. On a control chart, values between the upper and lower control limits result from random cause variation. When a control chart indicates variation only within the control limits, the process is considered to be "in statistical control." It is performing normally and results are predictable. Random cause variation cannot be isolated and identified. It can be eliminated only by analyzing and improving the whole process.

Special cause variation, sometimes called assignable cause variation, is not inherent in the process. It suggests that something different is acting on the system. An example might be an employee who suffered an eye injury during a weekend picnic. He is wearing a patch over one eye and seems to be doing well, but his temporarily impaired vision makes it difficult for him to read the medical claim forms accurately, resulting in occasional errors. On a control chart, values that lie outside the control limits result from special cause variation. When a control chart indicates values outside the control limits, the process is considered to be out of statistical control. The sources of special cause variation can and must be identified and eliminated to bring the process back into control. A process out of control will not produce predictable results and managers will have no idea about what to expect.

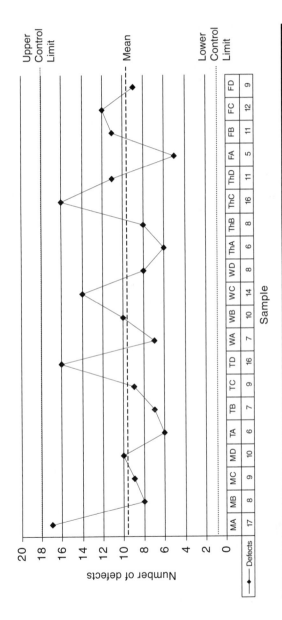

Figure 8.8. Control chart for medical claims review.

Exercise—Try this exercise as a demonstration of random cause and special cause variation. On a blank sheet of lined paper, write the capital letter "A" repeatedly along one line. Make all the letters look *exactly* alike. All the letters should be the same height, the angle between the sides should be the same, the horizontal line connecting the sides should be parallel with the line on the paper, and all horizontal lines should be exactly the same distance above the line on the paper. After you are finished, critically examine the result. Are all the letters *exactly* the same? Probably not, even though you tried your hardest to make them so. The miniscule differences result from random cause variation. You do not know what causes the differences; that is just the way it is.

Now prepare to write another line of letters just below the first. Make this second row look *exactly* like the first. But before you begin, move your pen or pencil to your other hand. After completing a line of letters, examine the results. Is the second row *exactly* like the first? Probably not. And is there a greater degree of variation among the letters in the second row? Probably so. The differences in the second row result from special cause variation. Something different was acting on the process. You changed hands and were now using your non-dominant hand to write the letters, causing a greater degree of variation.

Interpreting a control chart is rather simple. Data points that lie outside the control limits suggest special cause variation and require investigation. Data points that lie within the control limits suggest random cause variation and require no investigation, except for some unusual exceptions. In practice, evaluation is a little more complex than as described here. One additional thing to keep in mind is the "rule of seven." Seven consecutive data points progressing in one direction either up or down, or seven consecutive points on the same side of the mean, suggest that special cause variation is affecting the process even though the data points lie between the control limits. It is statistically unlikely that seven consecutive data points will occur in this manner. Such a situation should be investigated to determine if something is acting on the process and producing special cause variation.

Using control charts includes four steps:

1. **Collect** initial data. This will be the baseline data for the process.

2. **Create** the control chart. Plot the data. Calculate and plot the mean and the upper and lower control limits.

3. **Enter** new data. This is the key. A control chart is not just a snapshot of collected data. It is a tool for use over time to ensure that the process remains in statistical control. Using the mean and control limits established by the baseline data, enter new data points and determine if they lie within or outside the control limits.

4. **Do not change** the control limits based on new data unless the process changes. The control chart is the voice of the process. Do not try to change the voice unless you change the process. Completion of a process improvement effort to reduce random cause variation would be a reason to collect new data and establish a new mean and new control limits.

Control limits are established by data, not by management direction. A manager at JMS who is unfamiliar with control charts may look at the chart and decide that eighteen possible defective claim forms are too many. That manager might decide to establish the upper control limit at fifteen in an effort to improve performance. The intent is good, but the action is bad. Control charts define process performance; they are the voice of the process, but managers or customers may not be satisfied with process performance. Either may decide that they want to see fewer defects than indicated by the control charts. In so doing, they are establishing a specification that process performance is expected to meet. Specifications define customer requirements; they have been called the "voice of the customer."

Suppose JMS just received a letter from its largest client, an insurance company whose claims make up 60 percent of the claim form processing business. The client has expressed dissatisfaction with JMS's performance, citing an unacceptable level of complaints about processing times from its policyholders. The client has indicated that if performance does not improve, it will take its business elsewhere. JMS asks the project manager for advice.

The project manager understands that the insurance company does not have access to JMS performance data, so it could not provide a specific goal. It just wants things to be better. The project manager also realizes that major improvement may not occur overnight. She establishes a goal, a specification, of no more than fifteen defective reports in any sample of fifty as an initial target. She plots this specification on her control chart, as shown in Figure 8.9.

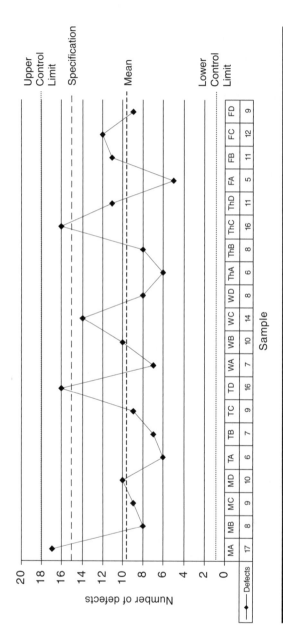

	MA	MB	MC	MD	TA	TB	TC	TD	WA	WB	WC	WD	ThA	ThB	ThC	ThD	FA	FB	FC	FD
Defects	17	8	9	10	6	7	9	16	7	10	14	8	6	8	16	11	5	11	12	9

Figure 8.9.   Control chart with specification.

The control chart now shows that the process is guaranteed to produce unacceptable results. The process is in control, it is performing predictably, but it is not performing according to specifications. It is producing a certain amount of unacceptable defects; that is, sixteen, seventeen, or eighteen defective claim forms per sample of fifty. The statistician informs the project manager that even the degree of defect is predictable—what percentage of the time defects of sixteen to eighteen will occur. When desired specification limits lie inside control limits, the process is considered to be in control, but not "capable." The statistician also informs the project manager that additional formulas are available to analyze process capability. The project manager decides that additional analysis is not necessary at this point. She works with the project team to prepare a recommended process improvement action for JMS that will identify and reduce sources of defects and change performance to the degree that any sample of fifty may be expected to include less than fifteen defective reports. The goal is to improve process performance, then collect new data that will show a new mean and new control limits that lie *within* specification limits, guaranteeing acceptable process performance.

The project manager did not recommend that JMS send its slickest salesperson over to the client to convince them to accept JMS's current performance. When there is a difference between the voice of the process (what the control chart reflects) and the voice of the customer (what the specification reflects), the voice of the process must always be changed to match the voice of the customer. The process must always be improved to meet customer specifications and expectations. Some may be tempted to "sell the client" the current process, to convince the client that it is as good as it can be, that the client must accept current performance. Such an approach eventually fails. Any initial agreement fades over time as frustration and dissatisfaction continue. Dissatisfied customers eventually seek other sources.

Control charts may be constructed quickly using a shortcut for determining the control limits. Recall from the discussion of Six Sigma in Chapter 3 that three standard deviations (3σ) above and below the mean account for 99.73 percent of the data under a normal curve. A quick way to create a control chart is to plot the data, plot the mean, and then set the control limits at 3σ above and below the mean. These control limits encompass 99.73 percent of the data, close enough to 100 percent for quality management purposes. Standard deviation may be easily calculated from the collected data using any handheld calculator with resident statistical functions. This method may not be as precise as the more rigorous methods that use more complex formulas. For example, the rigorous method applied to medical claim form data produced an upper control limit of 18.41. The 3σ method applied to the same data produces an upper control limit of 20.45. Wider control limits suggest a greater number of normal errors, which could be misleading to those seeking process improvement because more data are accepted as random cause variation. The rigorous methods are not very complex. They should be applied when possible.

Summary

◆ Flow charts identify the sequence of events in a process. They allow analysis of where errors might occur. A small set of commonly used symbols provides significant capability.

◆ Run charts show process performance over time. They are applied to repeatable processes in which results are expected to be consistent. Run charts show how data vary around a centerline, usually a mean.

◆ Control charts also show performance over time. They are run charts with added upper and lower control limits that allow monitoring, controlling, and improving processes over time.

◆ Control charts use sample data. Eight different types of control charts may be applied to process analysis. The type of chart is determined by the type of data and sample size.

◆ Control limits may be established through rigorous mathematical calculations or by setting them equal to 3σ above and below the mean.

◆ Data that lie within control limits result from random cause variation. This kind of variation is inherent in the system and can be reduced only by improving the whole process. When all data lie within control limits, the process is in statistical control and results are predictable.

◆ Data that lie outside control limits result from special cause variation. This kind of variation can and must be identified and removed to bring the process back into statistical control.

◆ Managers or customers may establish specification limits for process performance. If the specification limit is inside the control limit, the process is guaranteed to produce defective results. Processes must be improved so that control limits are inside specification limits, guaranteeing acceptable process performance.

Points to Ponder

1. How do flow charts help in understanding processes? Should a good flow chart be very broad or more narrow in scope? Should a flow chart be comprehensive or just cover the basics?
2. What information do run charts disclose? Why is this helpful in understanding processes?
3. Discuss the purpose and usefulness of control charts. What does "in control" mean? What is the difference between the voice of the process and the voice of the customer? How are each one displayed on a control chart? For extra credit, do a little research and describe the purpose and usefulness of different types of charts (there are eight).

Exercises

1. Prepare a flow chart for a common process with which you have personal knowledge or experience.
2. Prepare a run chart for a common activity in which you have personal knowledge or experience, e.g., daily commute either by conveyance or on foot, daily expenditures for lunch, daily outside temperature for 10 days, and so on.
3. If possible, collect some data on a repeatable process in which you are involved and prepare a control chart. Use the type of chart described in this chapter with the associated number and type of data points.

9

Analyzing
Project Processes

Having achieved an understanding of data and processes, project managers are ready to analyze processes and solve problems. Merely understanding a process is not a sufficient basis for taking action. Action without analysis is limited to precedent, intuition, trial and error, or guesswork about what the boss wants. None of these approaches is likely to yield happy results. Analysis is necessary to determine the system interaction aspects of the process and cause-effect relationships.

Tools for Analyzing Processes

Two tools are helpful in analyzing processes. One is a classic tool, proven over many years of effective use; the other is new.

Cause and Effect Diagrams

This diagram is sometimes called a "fishbone diagram" because of its shape and sometimes called an "Ishikawa diagram" in honor of its developer, Dr. Kaoru Ishikawa. It is used to identify, explore, and graphically display all possible causes related to a problem, including root causes. Using a cause and effect diagram includes four steps:

1. **Identify and define** the problem. Determine the extent of the problem to be addressed. It is important to establish specific and limited

boundaries that will focus the analysis and avoid an overly broad approach that may include multiple problems.

2. **Identify** major categories for causes. Causes constitute a unique set for individual problems. General models for causes may be useful as a start (for example, people, policies, procedures, and equipment), but each analysis effort must consider causes relevant to the specific problem, not simply a predefined set that may well be incomplete.

3. **Decompose** major causes down several levels. Carefully analyze each cause and determine what aspects or elements within that category might contribute to the problem being analyzed. Then analyze each aspect or element to determine what sub-elements might contribute to the problem. Then analyze each sub-element, and so on until the project team is comfortable that analysis is complete.

4. **Identify** root causes. Review the diagram and identify multiple occurrences of causes. For example, in a diagram with four categories, the sub-element "budget" may occur at several levels within each category. Multiple occurrences indicate a root cause; that is, a single cause that has many instances of effect throughout the process.

A basic model for cause and effect diagrams is shown in Figure 9.1. The image shows why the diagram is sometimes called a fishbone diagram. The problem identified in the box on the right is the head of the fish. The centerline is the backbone of the fish, and the lines that connect the category boxes to the centerline are the ribs.

As an example of applying the model, consider the matter of charge code number errors in monthly status reports. This was the most prevalent source of error identified in the check sheet and Pareto chart shown previously. Because this source offers the greatest opportunity for improvement, the project team decides to address it first. The team establishes "charge code number errors" as the problem and identifies four categories of possible cause:

1. **People**—Human error may be a contributing source.
2. **Policies**—Requirements established by management may also contribute.
3. **Procedures**—The manner in which policies are carried out may generate errors.
4. **Equipment**—The computers and other aspects of automated and manual systems may contribute to errors.

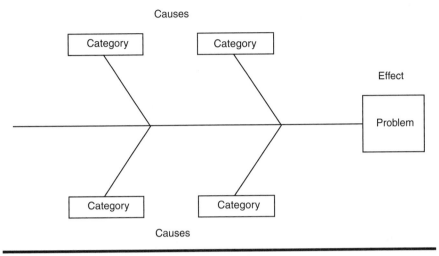

Figure 9.1.   Cause and effect diagram model.

The team sets up a cause and effect diagram framework as the first step in analysis (see Figure 9.2). The real work—and the real benefit—comes next as the team analyzes one category at a time and decomposes it down several levels of cause. The team focuses on each category individually and does not jump from category to category, as possible inter-category relationships might arise. The goal is complete and deep analysis of possible causes within categories. Figure 9.3 shows the decomposition of the "people" category.

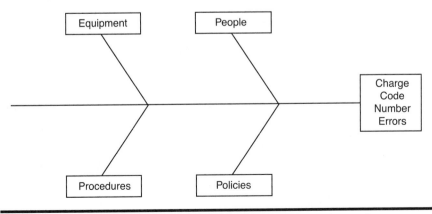

Figure 9.2.   Cause and effect diagram to analyze charge code number errors.

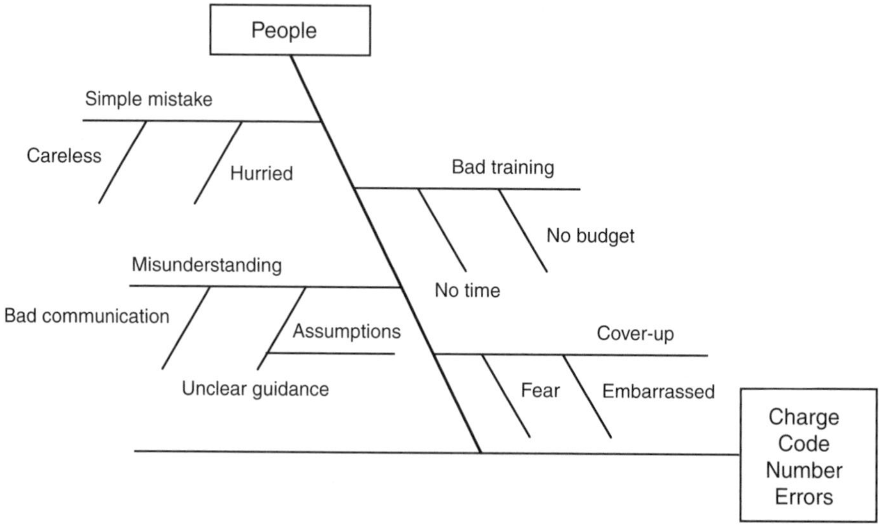

Figure 9.3. Decomposition of "people" category in a cause and effect diagram.

The project team first analyzed the "people" category to determine what people issues might be a cause of charge code number errors. They identified four possible causes: simple mistakes, bad training, misunderstandings, and cover-ups. Continuing the decomposition process, the team examined each one of these four causes and identified possible causes for each:

1. **Simple mistakes**—People could be careless and unintentionally enter a wrong number, perhaps by striking the wrong key on the keyboard when entering data into the automated accounting system. Or people could be rushed and make errors when trying to accomplish the data entry too quickly.
2. **Bad training**—It may be that people never completed essential training because they had no available time to attend training. Or perhaps training was never offered because funds were not available.
3. **Misunderstandings**—People may have used and reported erroneous charge codes because they misunderstood exactly what code they were allowed to use. Or they may have received unclear guidance and used the code they thought was most appropriate.

4. **Cover-ups**—People may have made errors and knew they made errors, but did not report and correct the errors because they were embarrassed by their mistake or afraid of being punished.

Then, continuing decomposition, the team looks at each one of the newly identified causes and identifies possible causes for it. Figure 9.3 shows that unclear guidance, which may be a cause of misunderstandings, may be caused by people making assumptions about what other people know.

As decomposition continues in all categories, the diagram becomes more complex and can become rather messy. The team should start the effort with sufficient space available for several levels of decomposition. If the team uses standard flip-chart paper, it might rotate the diagram ninety degrees counterclockwise and place the problem statement—the head of the fish—at the top of the paper. This allows a little more physical space for decomposition. Or the team might first make up an indented list, then draw the diagram. An indented list for the effort so far in the "people" category might look something like this:

Simple mistake
   Careless
   Hurried
Bad training
   No time
   No budget
Misunderstanding
   Bad communication
   Unclear guidance
     Assumptions
Cover-up
   Embarrassment
   Fear

Some teams find it easier to prepare an indented list first, then draw the diagram. This approach allows the team to probe and explore—to go back and forth, to add and delete—before putting the results on paper as a final diagram.

After the diagram is complete, the team reviews it, looking for repeated entries. Multiple occurrences suggest root causes. If, for example, "no budget" occurs in multiple locations across all categories, a lack of funding may be a root cause that, if eliminated, will have significant improvement effect on the problem being analyzed. Beyond root causes, the project team now has a comprehensive view of how things can go wrong. This information may be a basis for further focused data collection or a foundation for corrective action.

> **Exercise 1**—Your company is hosting a regional conference on behalf of a national technical association. The last time your company did this, it was a total disaster. Nothing went right. Participants were not happy and company management was not happy. Your boss has assigned you as project manager for this conference. He expects you to do a better job and conduct a flawless event. To analyze what went wrong with the previous conference, you decide to meet with a number of people who were involved and prepare a cause and effect diagram. Take some time right now and construct the diagram using your personal experience and imagination about what could go wrong in hosting a technical conference. The result in the diagram is "unsuccessful conference." Consider the following categories, or perhaps others: location, facilities, transportation, program, speakers, food service, proceedings, and administration. Try decomposing some categories graphically and others by indented list. Analyze the diagram and determine root causes. (There is no prescribed solution for this exercise.)

Pillar Diagrams

A cause and effect diagram is a powerful tool for analyzing a single problem and identifying all the possible causes. Sometimes a project team may want to analyze a situation in which multiple problems are related to multiple causes, all of which are generally known or can be identified readily and exist in limited number. A pillar diagram (a new quality tool introduced here for the first time) allows a project team to do just that. A pillar diagram is a combination of a cause and effect diagram and another quality tool, the interrelationship digraph. It addresses multiple problems (a cause and effect diagram addresses just one) and it shows relationships among a limited set of causes and results. An interrelationship digraph is used to determine relationships among all contributing elements of a system. The purpose of a pillar diagram is to identify root causes related to multiple results. To create a pillar diagram:

1. **Build** the pillars by identifying results, then causes. Results and causes are represented by boxes stacked on top of one another, resembling a pillar.
2. **Connect** causes to relevant results using arrows. Analyze each cause against each result in successive pair-wise comparisons. If there is a relevant relationship from the cause to the result, connect the cause box to the result box with an arrow.
3. **Count** the "out" arrows for each cause.
4. **Identify** root causes. Causes with the most arrows are root causes; that is, causes that influence the most results.

An example of how a pillar diagram might be used to analyze multiple causes and results related to late monthly status reports is shown in Figure 9.4.

To build the chart, the project team first determined what results would be analyzed. From the previously prepared check sheet and Pareto chart, the team

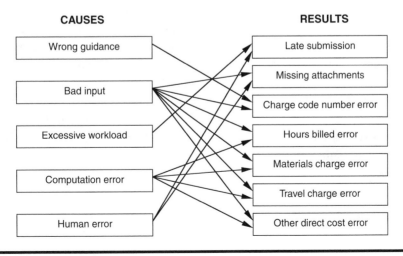

Figure 9.4. Pillar diagram for late monthly status reports.

decided to consider errors related to billing or payment. Errors related to charge code numbers and charges for labor, travel, materials, and other direct costs generate billing errors. Late submissions or missing attachments may cause the report to be returned for correction and delay payment. The team determined that errors related to date, period covered, and number of copies may have been one-time errors and did not include these in the pillar diagram analysis.

Next, the team considered what possible causes might be affecting the process. They identified the five causes shown in Figure 9.4. Then they analyzed each cause against each result and determined if a causal relationship existed between the two. If a relationship seemed apparent, they drew an arrow from the cause to the result. Counting the number of "out" arrows for each cause showed that two causes, bad input and computation errors, seemed to have the most influence on results and were, therefore, root causes. Process improvement actions to remove these two causes should produce significant improvement in performance.

The pillar diagram does not allow deep analysis of cause. It is not a decomposition tool like the cause and effect diagram. Subsequent analysis using a cause and effect diagram may be necessary before taking effective improvement action. For example, it may be necessary to analyze "bad input" further to identify root causes within that cause. Charge code and billing data for the monthly status report are not collected from original sources. They are taken from the monthly invoice already prepared by the accounting office. This ensures consistency between the invoice and the monthly status report. Any errors in the invoice are transferred directly to the monthly status report. The invoice may be identified as a source of input error, but further analysis will be necessary to determine the sources of erroneous invoice data. A cause and effect diagram would be an ideal tool for this additional analysis.

When analyzing causes, sometimes the degree of influence is more important than the number of results affected. It may be that all causes are of generally equal influence, but "wrong guidance" is far more influential because it sets in motion multiple billing errors that occur because of a basic charge code number error. When degree of influence is a concern, weights may be assigned to cause-result relationships as follows:

1 = low influence

3 = moderate influence

9 = high influence

This hierarchy of 1, 3, and 9 is drawn from a comprehensive quality tool called quality function deployment. The value of 3 should be used as a base, with cause-result relationships determined to be less influential assigned a value of 1 and cause-result relationships determined to be more influential assigned a value of 9. The values of "out" arrows for each cause should be added together and the sum divided by the total value of all arrows. The result is a percentage of influence for each cause that may, in some cases, identify root causes that are different from those identified by the number of relationships (arrows) alone. Now, a high percentage rather than a high number of arrows suggests root causes, those that have the greatest influence on results.

This method of applying a pillar diagram addresses the value of causes. It does not address the value of results. That is a different issue and should be addressed with different tools, perhaps a Pareto chart in which the defects are considered by their value rather than their number, as explained earlier.

Summary

- ◆ Analyzing processes is an essential step before taking improvement action.
- ◆ A cause and effect diagram is used to identify, explore, and graphically display all possible causes related to a single problem. It is sometimes called a fishbone diagram because of its distinctive shape or an Ishikawa diagram in honor of its inventor.
- ◆ A cause and effect diagram includes several categories of causes, determined by the problem being analyzed. Basic categories useful to project managers for analyzing processes include people, policies, procedures, and equipment. Categories are decomposed down several levels in a tree-like structure.
- ◆ In a cause and effect diagram, multiple occurrences of a single cause suggest it is a root cause. Eliminating root causes will have significant improvement effect across the process.
- ◆ Cause and effect diagrams may be constructed graphically or may be prepared first as an indented list, with the graphic being constructed after all causes have been identified.
- ◆ A pillar diagram is a new quality tool that may be used to identify root causes related to multiple results.

- ◆ A pillar diagram is created by graphically stacking multiple results and causes in columns that resemble pillars. Causes are then analyzed against each result. If a relationship exists, arrows are drawn from the cause to the result.
- ◆ Causes with the highest number of "out" arrows are the most significant causes, those that have the most influence on results.
- ◆ If cause-result relationships have different degrees of influence on a process, a pillar diagram may be constructed with weights of 1, 3, or 9 assigned to relationships to reflect low, moderate, or high influence, respectively.
- ◆ Pillar diagrams address causes and their influence on results. They do not address the value of results.

Points to Ponder

1. What is the purpose of cause and effect diagrams? Why are they useful? How are cause categories selected? How is data developed and analyzed?
2. What kinds of situations suggest the use of pillar diagrams? What is the outcome of applying a pillar diagram?

Exercises

1. One of the members of your class or perhaps a friend is having a birthday next month. You and several others would like to throw a party. The last time you did this, it did not go well. Prepare a cause and effect diagram to analyze a "bad birthday party." Generate your own list of possible causes. Your list may include things like location, entertainment, gifts, guests, food, and so on. Fill in the various branches of the "fishbone." Present your result to the class or to a collaborative work group.
2. Identify some kind of task or activity with which you have personal knowledge or experience that may include multiple problems arising from multiple causes. Prepare a pillar diagram to analyze the situation. Consider adding weighted values as described in this chapter.

10

Solving Project Problems

Collecting data, understanding and analyzing data, and analyzing processes are important. They are important as preparatory steps for taking action. These steps alone do not guarantee quality. Eventually, a project manager must do something. Much anecdotal guidance exists regarding action. The following may be familiar to many.

- ◆ "Do something. Even if it's wrong, do something." (A bias for action.)
- ◆ "It's better to ask for forgiveness than to ask for permission." (Do not wait for approval from others; act now.)
- ◆ "If you understand 80 percent of a problem, you have enough information to act." (Do not procrastinate. You will never have complete information.)

Taking action is necessary and good. Not taking the right action can lead to the classic excuse "It seemed like a good idea at the time."

Tools for Solving Problems

Four quality tools help a project manager determine the right action. Taken together, these tools constitute a progressive set that supports understanding of the organizational environment and supports generating, organizing, and prioritizing actions.

Force Field Analysis

Kurt Lewin (pronounced la-*veen*) was a social psychologist who was active and highly influential in the United States during the 1940s. He developed T-groups (the foundation for contemporary team building) and the "unfreeze-movement-refreeze" model of organizational change. He also developed force field analysis, a disciplined way of identifying forces and factors that help or hinder problem solving.

In Lewin's view, powerful forces that influence change are at play within any organization. These forces are of two types: those that help or enable change and those that hinder or restrain change. If you want to effect some kind of change within an organization, you must first identify and understand the forces at play and then use them in some advantageous way. Force field analysis is a method for doing this that includes five steps:

1. **Define** the challenge. Establish the scope of the analysis. The challenge may be very broad or it may be specific.
2. **Identify** helping and hindering forces. Consider the organization's operating environment. Determine what aspects of the environment might push the organization toward change and what aspects might stand as barriers to change.
3. **Assume** the forces are in balance. The opposing forces that may help or hinder change are probably in a state of equilibrium. That is why the organization is where it is at the current time; the forces that influence change are balanced.
4. **Develop** action plans to change the balance of forces. Changing the balance of opposing forces will break the equilibrium and allow change to occur.
5. **Change** the balance. Take the actions planned and pursue the desired change.

Force field analysis employs a simple graphic tool to organize the steps and capture the information for use. The example shown in Figure 10.1 addresses an organizational change—improving the quality of monthly status reports.

The challenge is entered at the top of the chart. Helping and hindering forces are entered in two columns below. Forces are entered in no particular order and there is no relationship between forces that may be listed across from each other on the chart. When forces are entered on the chart, they are

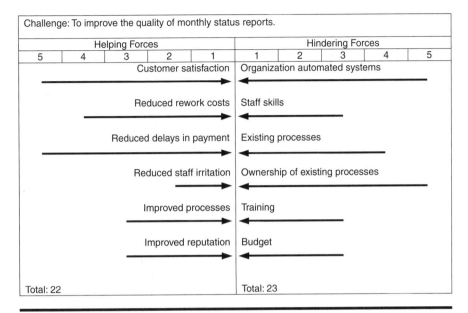

Challenge: To improve the quality of monthly status reports.									
Helping Forces					Hindering Forces				
5	4	3	2	1	1	2	3	4	5

Challenge: To improve the quality of monthly status reports.

Helping Forces					Hindering Forces				
5	4	3	2	1	1	2	3	4	5
Customer satisfaction →					Organization automated systems				
Reduced rework costs →					Staff skills				
Reduced delays in payment →					Existing processes				
Reduced staff irritation →					Ownership of existing processes				
Improved processes →					Training				
Improved reputation →					Budget				
Total: 22					Total: 23				

Figure 10.1. Force field analysis of monthly status report quality.

assigned a value from one to five, with one meaning "not too influential" and five meaning "very influential." The values are determined by the project team, either by consensus or simply by the judgment of the individual who suggested the force.

When all forces have been identified and added to the chart, the values are added together to create a total. Totals for helping and hindering forces need not be equal or close to equal. Those applying force field analysis should not juggle the values to create an artificial equivalence. The totals are just a guide. In fact, the values are just guides; their relevance will be apparent shortly. Recall that the forces are assumed to be in balance. All the forces that help or enable change are balanced by forces that hinder or restrain change, so no change is possible.

To make change possible, the influence of the forces must be altered in some way to either increase the influence of the helping forces or decrease the influence of the hindering forces. The result will be an imbalance of forces that will allow change. Often, the most effective approach is to reduce the influence of the hindering forces, which naturally allows the helping forces to be more influential even though they have not changed. Trying to increase the influence of helping forces (enhancing positives) can be difficult as such efforts can encounter resistance to change among organizational elements and members. On the other hand, decreasing the influence of hindering forces (decreasing negatives) usually does not encounter much resistance from organizational elements or members.

To develop action plans, each force is analyzed to determine what might be done to alter its influence and how the result might change the value of the force. Consider the hindering forces shown in Figure 10.1:

◆ **Organization automated systems**—Systems could be improved to allow edit checks for data entry and to allow electronic transfer of data from one report to another without human intervention that might be a source of errors. (Reduce influence from five to three.)

◆ **Staff skills**—Training could be applied that would improve staff skills in making decisions about data to be entered and in using the automated systems. (Reduce influence from three to one.)

◆ **Existing processes**—Process improvement could be applied that would reduce the opportunity for errors and allow identifying errors before they go into a final report. (Reduce influence from four to one.)

◆ **Ownership of existing processes**—This is a nice way to describe the situation where people want to do what they want to do because it is their area of responsibility. It is a difficult situation to address. Perhaps an effort to broaden the view of organizational elements to the degree that people understand better how their piece contributes to the whole may be effective. (Reduce influence from five to four.)

◆ **Training**—Training is a hindering force because nobody has the time for it and nobody wants to pay for it. Management support and directive may make training an obligation rather than an option. (Reduce influence from three to one.)

◆ **Budget**—Everything has a cost, and the matter of who will bear the cost of improvement is not trivial. Management support can make dedicated funds available for essential improvement activities. (Reduce influence from three to one.)

The results of this analysis and planned actions are shown in Figure 10.2 by the dashed-line arrows. The total value of the influence of the hindering forces is now eleven rather than twenty-three. This is a significant decrease that will result in a corresponding increase in the influence of the helping

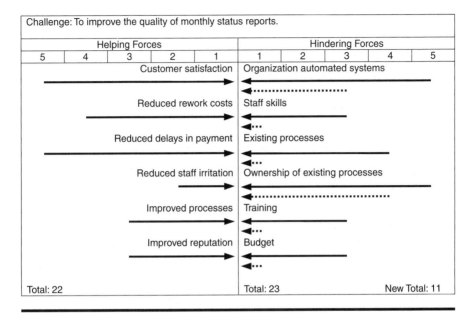

Figure 10.2. **Force field analysis: effect of improvement actions.**

forces. The result should be an overall ability to take effective change actions in areas related to helping forces because such action will not bump against balancing hindering forces that act to maintain the status quo. Note that the values assigned to the forces serve only as a guide. A planned action to reduce the hindering influence of staff skills may be expected to have beneficial effect that is expressed as a reduction of the influence level from three to one. The total value of eleven is only an expression of the degree of improvement. It shows that the balance of helping-hindering forces has changed significantly; the forces are no longer in balance and change should be possible.

> **Exercise 1**—Consider the challenge "improve organization quality" and conduct a force field analysis using your own work experience. Prepare a chart as described above. (There is no prescribed solution for this exercise.)

Brainstorming

Brainstorming is a common quality tool that is much applied in the breach. That is, people think they are doing brainstorming, but they are really just having a discussion. True brainstorming is a formal process that may be applied in a structured or unstructured approach, as described below. The goal of either method is to generate a high volume of ideas creatively and efficiently, free of criticism and other chilling or disruptive influences.

Structured Approach

- ◆ **Step 1**. The team meets in a location that provides some privacy, free from interruption. The location should have comfortable seating and either writing boards on the wall or flip charts on stands. The team decides on a scribe who will write down the ideas as they are generated during the brainstorming session.
- ◆ **Step 2**. The project team identifies and defines the issue to be addressed. The scribe enters this on the board or flip chart.
- ◆ **Step 3**. Team members present ideas, going around the team in round-robin fashion. Each team member presents only one idea. Then it is the next member's turn. The scribe writes the idea on the board or flip chart.
  - ◊ **Note**: No criticism, clarification, prioritization, or discussion of any kind is allowed. Any of these may disrupt the flow and possibly bog down the team in fruitless, wandering discussion.
- ◆ **Step 4**. Team members may "pass" if they do not have an idea when their turn comes around. This does not exclude them from further participation. Intervening ideas presented by others may stimulate thought that may generate an idea on the next go-round.
- ◆ **Step 5**. When all team members pass in succession, the idea generation is over. The team may now review the ideas generated and clarify any fine points or perhaps remove duplicates. Teams should exercise great care in removing any ideas from the list as duplicates. What may seem like duplication may, in fact, be a different idea based on a nuance of meaning of the suggester.
- ◆ **Step 6**. After tidying up the list, the brainstorming session is finished, with the result being a list of ideas that address the subject issue.

Unstructured Approach

- ◆ **Step 1.** The team meets in a location that provides some privacy, free from interruption. The location should have comfortable seating and either writing boards on the wall or flip charts on stands. The team decides on a scribe who will write down the ideas as they are generated during the brainstorming session.

♦ **Step 2**. The project team identifies and defines the issue to be addressed. The scribe enters this on the board or flip chart.

♦ **Step 3**. Team members call out ideas as the ideas occur to them. There is no need to wait their turn. Members are not limited in the number of ideas they may present at one time. If someone has twenty ideas and can get them all out without taking a breath, so be it. The scribe writes the ideas on the board or flip chart, trying to keep up with the flow of ideas.

  ◊ **Note**: No criticism, clarification, prioritization, or discussion of any kind is allowed. Any of these may disrupt the flow and possibly bog down the team in fruitless, wandering discussion. This constraint may be harder to observe in the unstructured approach because of the free-for-all aspect of participation.

♦ **Step 4**. Eventually, everyone will run out of ideas. When the participation is clearly finished, not just at a lull, the idea generation is over. This point should be determined by team consensus, not by direction of one particular participant.

♦ **Step 5**. The team may now review the ideas generated and clarify any fine points or perhaps remove duplicates. Teams should exercise great care in removing any ideas from the list as duplicates. What may seem like duplication may, in fact, be a different idea based on a nuance of meaning of the suggester.

♦ **Step 6**. After tidying up the list, the brainstorming session is finished, with the result being a list of ideas that address the subject issue.

The two approaches, structured and unstructured, offer different advantages and disadvantages. A structured approach allows everyone to take a turn and prevents one person from monopolizing the session. It allows time for individual thought and reflection as participants await their next turn. It may produce better-formed ideas. A structured approach may also make people participate who otherwise might sit silently by as others generate all the ideas. Those who might be rather reserved or who might feel that nobody listens to their ideas anyway now have a dedicated time in the spotlight, a time when they hold the floor and everyone else is obligated to listen. The disadvantage is that this very deliberate approach may not release creative energy. It may give people a chance to "think twice" and offer more cautious ideas or even withhold ideas that, in a more spontaneous approach, they would throw out for consideration. All participants must keep in mind that creativity is a common rule in both approaches. No idea is too wild, too silly, or too unconventional for consideration.

The unstructured approach allows an element of spontaneity and may result in more creative ideas. People are not restricted to waiting their turn and, as a result, things can get a bit raucous. This is good. It may be just what is needed to break the bonds of conventional thinking and open the doors to new ideas, no matter how wild and crazy they may seem initially. With no control on who speaks when, the potential exists that one especially gregarious or perhaps overbearing individual may monopolize the session. In practice, this is seldom the case. Even when they are on a rant, people run out of steam. Given the unconstrained nature of the session, a slight pause is all other participants need to jump in with their own ideas. Rules of decorum and courtesy should be relaxed without offense to allow an energetic, free flow of ideas.

The greater danger (and the greatest disadvantage) of the unstructured approach is that the session might degenerate into a meandering discussion. People who are free to jump in any time with new ideas may feel free to criticize or comment on ideas suggested by others. After all, there are no rules, right? Wrong. The team must decide up front and agree throughout the session to observe the rule about no criticism, clarification, prioritization, or discussion during idea generation.

The results of both approaches are generally the same: a list of ideas. Ideas generated through the structured approach may be better defined. Ideas generated through the unstructured approach may be more creative. In practice, the number of ideas generated by either approach is about the same. So which approach should a team use? It depends on the preference of the team. If team members are more deliberate and reserved in their personal interactions, a structured approach may be better. If team members tend to be quick to respond and are more outgoing in their personal interaction, an unstructured approach may be better. The team should decide among itself what approach to use in brainstorming.

> **Exercise 2**—Within your own project team, find an excuse to generate some ideas about an issue using the brainstorming techniques described here. Try both a structured approach and an

unstructured approach. Explain the difference to the team ahead of time. After you have tried both, discuss the experiences within the team. Decide if one works better than the other. Decide if the ideas generated are different or better than the kinds of ideas generated through usual team practice if that usual practice differs from the techniques described here.

Affinity Diagrams

You must remember this: A list is just a list. Having generated a list of ideas through brainstorming, the project team must now make some sense out of it. Ideas are probably listed helter-skelter on the board or flip chart in the order that they were generated. An affinity diagram is a quality tool that is used to organize and summarize unstructured issues or ideas. Recall the task manager, who just received another "see me" note from the project manager.

TM: Hey Bob ...

PM: Jim, you need to do something for me, and quick. When the corporate quality director was here last week—you were on the site visit that day—she said she wanted some ideas from the trenches on how to improve quality. So she had a brainstorming session with your team ...

TM: Yeah, I heard ...

PM: ... that generated this list of ideas. Well, she took it with her and I thought that was the end of it. Then I get this note from the program manager that says he got the list from the VP for operations. He attached the list and asked me what I'm doing about it. Hey ... it's just a list of ideas that go all over the place. I don't even know what it means, let alone what to do about it.

TM: Relax, Bob. I know this hit you cold, but I've got a quality tool that is just perfect for this. It's called an affinity diagram. I can see you are really pressed here. I'll go see what my people are up to and try to get back to you in a couple of hours with some answers.

PM: Good! Go!

The list the task manager received was the classic output from a brainstorming session: a list of widely differing ideas with no suggestion of order (see Table 10.1). The task manager looks over the list and notices some things

Table 10.1.   Brainstorming Results: How to Improve Quality.

1. Improve leadership
2. Get better requirements
3. Develop a training plan
4. Make rewards fair
5. Improve senior management skills
6. Improve project management
7. Develop a project management methodology
8. Increase training budget
9. Train new hires
10. Listen to employees
11. Solicit employee suggestions
12. Follow established procedures
13. Develop training for new processes
14. Send managers to training
15. Stop punishing honest mistakes
16. Improve performance controls
17. Stop the training "guilt trip"

that he has found that are typical of brainstorming results. The early ideas are very broadly stated. The ideas toward the middle get a little bolder, they even show a little frustration, and the ideas at the end are rather blunt. He checks with the team and discovers that everyone is available for a short meeting. He assembles the team in the conference room and explains that an affinity diagram is a quality tool for organizing and summarizing unstructured ideas and issues, exactly the tool to apply to the brainstorming list to try and make some sense of it. He explains the five steps of the affinity diagramming process:

1. **Write** each idea on a "sticky note" (a small note-size piece of paper with a lightly adhesive back) and stick all the notes on the wall or a flip chart.
2. **Move** notes into groups with some kind of association. Team members do this in incremental steps, one at a time. Team members do this silently, without discussion.
3. **Make** duplicate notes in cases of conflict among team members.
4. **Discuss** and resolve conflicts when all ideas have been grouped together in some way.

5. **Create** headers or titles for the groups that reflect the content of the ideas.

The team members get to work. They write each idea on a sticky note and paste it on the board in the conference room in no particular order or arrangement (see Figure 10.3).

The task manager asks the first team member to step to the board and move the notes to place any that seem to have some kind of connection or affiliation into a column. He tells her not to try and rearrange the whole list. Just move the notes that seem most obvious. She does that. Silently, without explanation or discussion among the team, she rearranges a few notes so the board now looks like Figure 10.4.

The task manager then invites the second team member to step to the board and try to make some associations among the tasks. She moves some notes so the board now looks like Figure 10.5.

The third team member steps to the board and confidently begins to move tasks associated with leadership into one column. He feels that the previous

Figure 10.3. Affinity diagram: random arrangement of ideas.

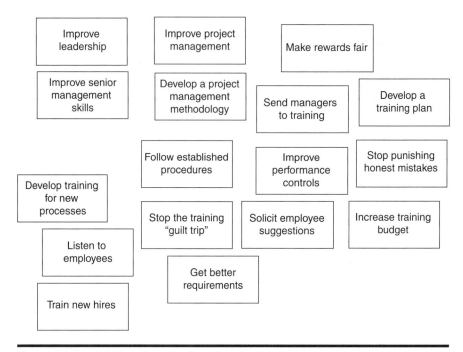

Figure 10.4. Affinity diagram: first round.

member made a mistake in grouping "send managers to training" with tasks that seem to be related to training because the important thing is the effect this task has on leadership. He starts to move the note when the task manager intervenes and explains that each team member's action is unchangeable; it cannot be undone or overruled by another member. If one team member feels that a task belongs in a group other than the one in which it was placed by another member, the dissenting team member makes a copy of the task and associates it with the other group. The third team member makes a copy of the "send managers to training" task and places it under the first column. The board now looks like Figure 10.6.

The task manager steps to the board and completes the affinity diagram by moving the remaining tasks into a column. The board now shows three columns of associated tasks (see Figure 10.7).

The task manager congratulates the team on the work thus far. He asks them to consider the columns of ideas that they have created. What is it about the ideas in each column that suggests an association? What is the common thread? With all the ideas in neat stacks, the team quickly decides that the

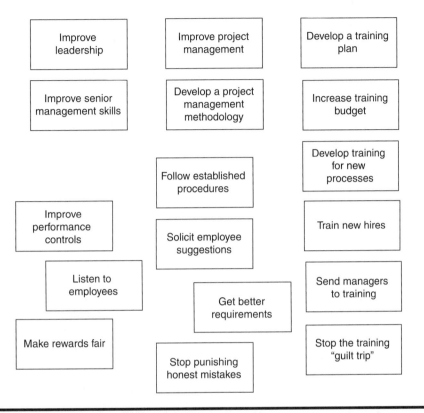

Figure 10.5. Affinity diagram: round two.

first column has something to do with leadership and management, the second column is about technical performance, and everything in the third column is related to training in some way. The task manager makes up three notes and sticks them at the top of the columns as titles (see Figure 10.8).

The task manager congratulates the team again. They started with a set of randomly generated and collected ideas and ended with an ordered grouping that discloses what is important to improving quality in the organization. He asks the team to stand by while he pays a brief visit to the project manager.

TM: Bob, I've got some initial information for you.

PM: Shoot.

TM: Take a look at this affinity diagram. (Shows him Figure 10.8.) It shows that all the ideas generated during the brainstorming session fall into three categories: leadership, technical performance, and training.

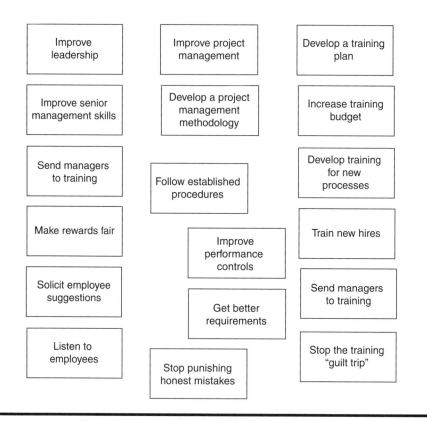

Figure 10.6.   Affinity diagram: round three.

PM: Now that I can understand. This is great!

TM: We aren't done yet. We have an ordered list, but it's still just a list. We can't do everything on the list at once and we don't know which ones we should do first, which ones are most important.

PM: Another tool, right?

TM: Yes. I've got the team standing by. I'll be back shortly to tell you what we do first.

Nominal Group Technique and Multivoting

Nominal group technique was developed at the University of Wisconsin in 1971 as a means of developing team consensus on priority rankings free of bias or influence. It is called "nominal" group technique because the teams

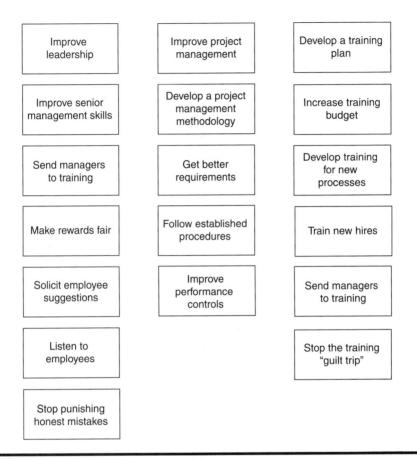

Figure 10.7.   Affinity diagram: round four.

that apply it are usually ad hoc groups that are temporary in nature and do not go through the building processes necessary to become a formal group in a sociological sense. It is a disciplined process, not a haphazard approach, which allows the collection of input in a way that overcomes group bias or social influence by others. It builds commitment through equal participation of team members.

Nominal group technique works best when the number of ideas under consideration is about fifty or less. More than fifty ideas may be too many for team members to grasp at one time. Recall the corporate quality director who conducted the brainstorming session that generated seventeen ideas. Suppose she had, instead, sent out a survey to a number of employees across

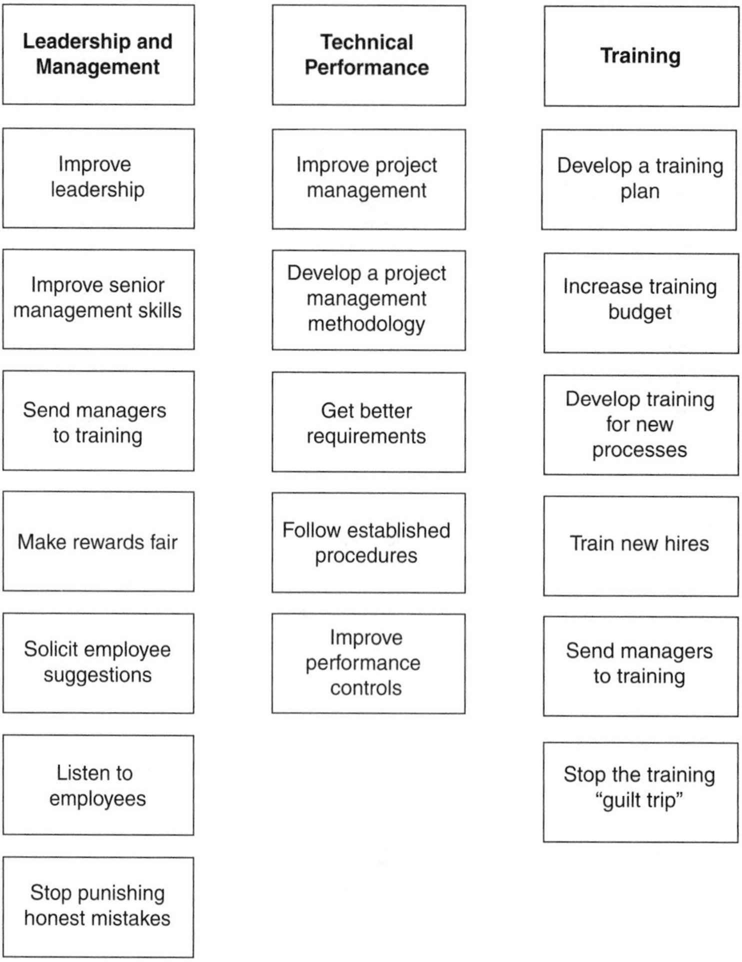

Leadership and Management	Technical Performance	Training
Improve leadership	Improve project management	Develop a training plan
Improve senior management skills	Develop a project management methodology	Increase training budget
Send managers to training	Get better requirements	Develop training for new processes
Make rewards fair	Follow established procedures	Train new hires
Solicit employee suggestions	Improve performance controls	Send managers to training
Listen to employees		Stop the training "guilt trip"
Stop punishing honest mistakes		

Figure 10.8.   Affinity diagram: final product.

the organization asking for five good ideas for improving quality. After receiving responses and eliminating duplicates, she may have a list of eighty or ninety ideas. She could reduce the number to fifty or less by assembling a small analysis team and applying multi-voting in the following way:

1. **List** all the ideas and assign a sequential number to each.
2. **Ask** each team member to identify the top twenty ideas from the list and write the numbers for those ideas on a sheet of paper. There

is nothing magical about the number twenty. It is just a nice round number that seems to work well in most cases. If the total number of ideas is larger (say, 125 or so), a number of thirty top-priority ideas may be more appropriate.

3. **Tabulate** the results. Collect the individual top-twenty lists and assign one point to each idea on the total list for each time it appears on an individual top-twenty list. Add the scores for each idea on the total list.

4. **Delete** ideas with low scores. Starting with ideas that received no points at all may be sufficient to reduce the list to fifty or less. If not, delete those with a score of one, then two, and so on until the list has been sufficiently reduced. All deletions should be done by group consensus. No idea should be deleted without permission of the originator.

Nominal group technique consists of five general steps, with some variation within the steps in practice:

1. **Generate** ideas. Team members, silently and on their own, write their ideas on a piece of paper. There is no limit on the number of ideas and no constraints on the nature of the ideas. As in brainstorming, creativity is the rule. Team members may write all ideas on a single sheet of paper or, if anonymous input is desired, they may write each idea on a separate note card, such as an index card.

2. **Collect** and record ideas. Each team member discloses one idea at a time, going around the team in round-robin fashion until all ideas have been disclosed. The team leader writes the ideas on a flip chart using as many pages as necessary. If the team desires anonymous input, the team leader collects the note cards, perhaps shuffling them to eliminate any order of collection that might suggest the writer's identity, and writes all the ideas on the flip chart.

3. **Review** and discuss the ideas. Remove any obvious duplicates, being careful not to eliminate ideas that are similar, but slightly different. Discuss each idea briefly to make sure everyone has the same understanding. The team leader must keep the discussion moving so that this step does not turn into a discussion or argument about the merits of the ideas. The purpose is clarification only.

4. **Vote** on the ideas. Each team member, individually and anonymously, selects and prioritizes a small number of ideas from the total
   list. In practice, the number selected varies. In one convention, team
   members select and prioritize five ideas from the total. In another
   convention, the number selected for prioritization depends on the total according to the following scale:
   - Up to twenty ideas, prioritize four
   - Twenty-one to thirty-five ideas, prioritize six
   - Thirty-six or more ideas, prioritize eight

   No matter the number of ideas, the prioritization process is the same.
   By convention, each team member writes the idea's sequential number in the upper left corner of a note card, then writes the idea in the
   center of the card. Team members place all the cards in front of them
   and rank-order them according to priority. They write the priority
   number in the lower right corner with priority values from highest
   to lowest. When prioritizing four ideas, the first priority is assigned
   a value of four, the second priority is assigned a value of three, the
   third priority is assigned two, and the fourth, one. The technique is
   the same when prioritizing six ideas, except it begins with a first priority value of six.

5. **Record** results. The team leader collects the cards, shuffles them
   to avoid disclosing a writer's identity, and enters the priority values
   from the cards on the general list. Adding all the priority numbers for
   each idea yields a prioritized list.

Recall the task manager who promised the project manager an answer as to
which of the seventeen ideas about quality improvement should be addressed
first. He went back to the team which was standing by and applied nominal
group technique to the list of seventeen ideas that had already been generated
by brainstorming. He gave each of the five team members four note cards
and asked them to select the top four priority ideas from the list of seventeen.
He asked them to write the idea number in the upper left corner of a card and
the idea in the center of the card. He then asked them to place all four cards
in front of them and arrange them in priority order, highest to lowest. Once
that was done, he asked them to write the priority numbers on the cards,
highest to lowest, four to one, in the lower right corner.

The task manager then had one team member collect the cards and shuffle them. He took the cards and wrote the priority numbers from each card beside the idea description on the total list. The results are shown in Table 10.2.

It was a simple matter of rewriting the list to produce a prioritized list shown in Table 10.3. The task manager now had the data he needed to go back to the project manager.

> TM: Bob, I've got an answer for you about what to do first on the quality list.
>
> PM: I suppose you're going to tell me we need more money and time for training so we can improve employee performance.
>
> TM: No. The answer is pretty obvious; it screams really. I used something called nominal group technique that allows prioritization free from bias or predisposition. Look at the results here. (Shows him Table 10.3.) Two things jump out. The things to do first are getting better requirements from our customers and developing a project management methodology.

Table 10.2. Results of Nominal Group Technique.

	Priorities	Total
1. Improve leadership	4	4
2. Get better requirements	4, 3, 3	10
3. Develop a training plan		0
4. Make rewards fair		0
5. Improve senior management skills	4	4
6. Improve project management		0
7. Develop a project management methodology	3, 2, 4	9
8. Increase training budget	4	4
9. Train new hires	1	1
10. Listen to employees	2, 1	3
11. Solicit employee suggestions		0
12. Follow established procedures	2, 1, 2	5
13. Develop training for new processes	3	3
14. Send managers to training	3	3
15. Stop punishing honest mistakes	1	1
16. Improve performance controls	1	1
17. Stop the training "guilt trip"	2	2

Table 10.3.   Quality improvement ideas prioritized by using nominal group technique.

	Priorities	Total
2. Get better requirements	4, 3, 3	10
7. Develop a project management methodology	3, 2, 4	9
12. Follow established procedures	2, 1, 2	5
1. Improve leadership	4	4
5. Improve senior management skills	4	4
8. Increase training budget	4	4
10. Listen to employees	2, 1	3
13. Develop training for new processes	3	3
14. Send managers to training	3	3
17. Stop the training "guilt trip"	2	2
9. Train new hires	1	1
15. Stop punishing honest mistakes	1	1
16. Improve performance controls	1	1
3. Develop a training plan		0
4. Make rewards fair		0
6. Improve project management		0
11. Solicit employee suggestions		0

PM: That makes sense. If we don't know what our customers want, the greatest performance in the world won't get it right. And if we know better what they want, we can still fail by inconsistent performance. I like it.

TM: And one more thing. Look at this idea that came up third: "Follow established procedures." It fits right in with the first two even though there is something of a break in the priority numbers. A good project management methodology won't be of any value if we don't follow the procedures. I think we have a good set here of three things to do right now and maybe look at some of the following priorities as we go along.

PM: Good work. I'll show this to the VP and see if I can break loose some funding for these actions. I'll let you know what happens.

Nominal group technique is a proven, powerful tool for prioritizing ideas without the bias of external influence. Because people generate ideas on their own, they are not likely to be led by others or intimidated by others. If potential intimidation is an issue, idea collection should be anonymous. Prioritization should always be anonymous. The result of applying nominal group technique is a prioritized list that represents group consensus, not just the desires of the aggressive or powerful.

Summary

◆ To solve problems, project managers must take action. Quality tools help determine the right action to take.

◆ Problem solving and quality improvement involve change. Before you can make a change of some kind, you must understand the forces at play within the organization that influence change.

◆ Force field analysis identifies forces and factors that help or hinder problem solving. Helping forces must be made more influential or hindering forces must be made less influential. It is often easier to reduce the influence of hindering forces than it is to increase the influence of helping forces.

◆ Brainstorming is a tool for creatively and efficiently generating a high volume of ideas free of criticism. During brainstorming, creativity is the rule; no idea is too unconventional for consideration. No criticism, clarification, prioritization, or discussion of ideas is permitted as ideas are presented.

◆ Brainstorming may be employed in a structured approach in which team members present one idea at a time, going around the team in round-robin fashion.

◆ Brainstorming may be employed in an unstructured approach in which team members present their ideas in a free-for-all fashion with no limit on the number of ideas presented at one time and no sequence of presentation among team members.

◆ The brainstorming approach employed depends on the desires and personalities of the team.

◆ An affinity diagram may be used to organize and summarize unstructured ideas or issues. Team members associate individual ideas with other ideas that have something in common one at a time until all ideas are grouped together in associated categories. Groups are then given titles that reflect the nature of the association.

◆ A large number of ideas may be reduced to a more workable number by multi-voting in which each team member assigns one point each to the top twenty ideas among the total. Adding all points for each idea allows elimination of low-scoring ideas. No idea should be eliminated without the writer's concurrence.

◆ Nominal group technique is a method for developing team consensus on priority ranking of ideas or issues free of bias or influence. Ideas may be generated by anonymous input from team members or by a public disclosure method such as brainstorming.

◆ In applying nominal group technique, team members anonymously assign priorities to a small number of ideas. Adding priorities for each idea produces a prioritized list that was reached by team consensus.

Points to Ponder

1. Discuss the purpose and usefulness of force field analysis. What is the basic principle? What is the basic goal?

2. Describe the two approaches to brainstorming. When might one be more useful than the other? What are some advantages and disadvantages of each approach?

3. How do affinity diagrams help make sense of large amounts of data? What source of knowledge do they tap into? How do they reduce bias?

4. Discuss the purpose and usefulness of nominal group technique and multi-voting. What is the purpose of multi-voting? What is the benefit of anonymous idea generation and voting?

Exercises

1. Identify a situation with which you are familiar that includes multiple contributing factors. Prepare a force field analysis chart that will allow you to develop a plan to improve the situation.

2. With a group of classmates or colleagues, conduct a brainstorming session using each of the two approaches. Did one work better than the other? Were you able to stick to the "rules of the road"?

3. Pick a moderately complex problem or situation with multiple contributing factors. On your own, identify a large number of

contributing factors. Organize them and make sense of them using an affinity diagram.

4. With a small group of classmates or colleagues, pick a problem or situation of moderate interest and analyze it using nominal group technique and multi-voting.

11

Common Project Practices

Managing project quality is not restricted to using traditional quality tools. Project managers may and should use or develop whatever tools are necessary to deliver quality products and services to customers.

Commonly Used Tools

The two tools described below are not among the set of traditional quality tools, but they are so ubiquitous in use that any discussion of project quality would be incomplete without mentioning them.

Compliance Matrix

A compliance matrix is a tool to ensure that actions comply with requirements. It may be a simple checklist or it may be a little more complex. Its first application to project quality may be during the bid and proposal phase. A good compliance matrix well applied will provide confidence that the proposal responds to all requirements in the solicitation. It may also be applied during project implementation as a checklist for deliverables. A good compliance matrix will ensure that all requirements have been met before a deliverable is released to the customer. Project managers may design the matrix structure in any way that meets project needs. An example format is shown in Figure 11.1. The example includes essential elements of information necessary to ensure compliance with requirements.

Ref	Requirement	Response	Done	Date	Contact

Figure 11.1.   Compliance matrix.

- ◆ **Reference**—This column shows the paragraph numbers of the requirements, perhaps from a solicitation document or a task order of some kind.
- ◆ **Requirement**—This column includes the exact requirements from the solicitation document or task order. Requirements may be extracted and quoted directly or they may be summarized in language that is meaningful to the project team. Either way, all requirements must be included. It may be useful to analyze the paragraphs in the source document and look for verbs. Any verb (action word) indicates that what follows is something that must be done. A verb tied to descriptive language constitutes a probable requirement.
- ◆ **Response**—In the simplest use of a compliance matrix, this column may include brief statements of what the project team will do to comply with the requirement. In an expanded use, perhaps during the bid and proposal phase, this column may be a repository of ongoing notes about how the project team will comply. When the matrix is complete, this column may then be used as a foundation for writing the final proposal.
- ◆ **Done**—This column indicates status on completion of the requirement-response connection as a yes/no entry.
- ◆ **Date**—This column indicates the date of completion or latest action.
- ◆ **Contact**—This column indicates contact data for the individual responsible for the action or individuals who must be included in coordination.

To show how a compliance matrix may be applied, consider the following extract from a request for proposal for the Dakota Wireless Network.

1. Mandatory requirements.
   a. Vendor will establish an operating location within twenty miles of Dakota Department of Communications headquarters.
   b. Excluding on-site installation, 80 percent of all work performed under this contract as measured by labor hours billed will be performed by vendor employees assigned to and working at the operating location.
   c. All vendor employees billing in "program manager" or "project manager" labor categories will hold a current Project Management Professional® (PMP®) certification from the Project Management Institute.

Note: Proposals not meeting all of the mandatory requirements will be viewed as non-responsive and given no further consideration.

Figure 11.2 shows how these requirements are entered into a compliance matrix.

The project team has analyzed the request for proposal and identified all requirements. The compliance matrix shows the paragraph number and a brief description of each requirement. It includes a bullet list of actions to be taken in response to comply with the requirements. Note that the project team

Ref	Requirement	Response	Done	Date	Contact
1.	Mandatory requirements				
1.a.	Establish operating location within 20 miles of DDOC	• Identify 3 possible locations • Establish non-binding letters of intent with property managers • Describe LOI in proposal • Attach LOI as appendix	no	8/18	G. Johns Ext: 5919
1.b.	80% of all work (less on-site installation) must be performed by employees at the Dakota operation location	• Assign sufficient staff to Dakota location • Report % of local hours billed in each monthly status report • Require Program Manager approval of all off-site work	no	8/18	J. Dewar Ext: 5205
1.c.	Anyone billing in Program or Project Manager labor category must be PMP certified	• Bid only PMP-certified PMs • Require PMP certification before future assignment as PM	yes	8/18	R. Fitts Ext: 5860

Figure 11.2.   Compliance matrix: Dakota Wireless Network.

cannot rent office space without a contract, but it can make arrangements for potential office space through non-binding letters of agreement with property managers. These agreements can be part of the proposal to show a good-faith effort to establish an operating location as required. The matrix also shows completion status and date. Item 1.c indicates "yes" because the project team has identified employees to bid as program or project managers and all hold a current PMP® certification. Last, the matrix shows the name and telephone number of the person responsible for completing the actions.

As a next step, the project team might select its most gifted writer to prepare the final proposal using the information in the "response" column as a guide. When the proposal has been written and coordinated, the compliance matrix might serve as a last-step checklist for reviewing the proposal before it is submitted to the soliciting organization.

Peer Review

Peer review is a common practice in most project organizations. Its purpose is to ensure technical soundness of products before they are delivered to customers. Products involved are usually plans, reports, or some other type of intellectual document. Peer review is a simple process. When authors complete documents, they send the finished product to another person who possesses technical expertise equal to or superior to their own. That person reviews the document for technical soundness. If reviewers disagree about approach, methods, conclusions, or any technical aspects of the documents, they work out the disagreement directly with the authors. If reviewers and authors cannot agree, they escalate the matter to a superior (a task manager or a project manager) for resolution.

Peer review is focused on technical matters only. It is not a review of grammar or writing style; that is an editorial review, which is an entirely different process. Peer reviewers must resist any temptation to force authors to "write it my way." At the same time, authors must be able to accept technical criticism and not defend on "that's the way I write." Peer review is an excellent way to get a second look at important products before they are delivered to customers.

Peer review can have a dark side. Some authors may funnel their documents to personal friends who are not likely to criticize their work or to other writers with whom they have an unspoken mutual non-critique agreement. This can lead to ineffective reviews and the phenomenon of "group think." Some reviewers may use the process to take cheap shots at authors with whom they may be feuding or whom they see as competitors for promotion, rewards, or influence within the organization. Effective peer review depends on good intentions by all, inoffensive candor by all involved, and non-punitive resolution of any technical disagreements.

Summary

- ◆ A compliance matrix is used to ensure that actions comply with requirements. It may be applied as a checklist or as a tool for developing a comprehensive, responsive proposal.
- ◆ Peer review is a common method of ensuring technical soundness of intellectual products prior to delivery to customers.
- ◆ Peer review is technically focused. It is not a review of grammar or writing style.

Points to Ponder

1. How may a compliance matrix be used as a simple checklist? How may it be used in a more extensive way?
2. Describe the purpose and usefulness of peer review. What are the benefits? What are the potential pitfalls?

Exercises

1. From some convenient public source (local business, government, professional associations), obtain a request for proposal. Keep it small. Prepare a compliance matrix up to the point of writing an actual proposal.
2. With a few classmates or colleagues you trust—and in a non-competitive and non-punitive environment—share some actual work papers and conduct a peer review.

Section IV

Quality in Practice

12

Project Systems
and Solutions

Project quality is a result of many things working together to produce a satisfied customer. Things that work together constitute a system. To manage project quality, project managers must, in Dr. Deming's words, gain an appreciation for systems. They must understand the elements of the system within which they work and how the elements interact with and influence each other. This is no easy task. System performance can be obscured by arrogance, ignorance, or bias. To overcome these hurdles, Dr. Deming developed a demonstration using red and white beads.

The Red Bead Experiment

Dr. Deming explained the red bead experiment in his book *Out of the Crisis*. He also credited William A. Boller of the Hewlett-Packard Company with introducing the demonstration at a company seminar. The experiment includes the following:

- **People**—Six workers, consistently referred to as "willing workers"; two inspectors and one chief inspector; and one recorder.
- **Materials**—Red and white spherical beads (commercially available demonstration kits generally provide 4000 beads: 3200 white, 800 red), a container to hold the beads, and a paddle with fifty indentations that will hold one bead each.

◆ **Processes**—Willing workers dip the paddle into the bead container until it is completely covered, then carefully withdraw it. Gently shaking the paddle and allowing excess beads to roll off results in a paddle with a bead in each of the fifty indentations.

During the experiment, each willing worker, in turn, dips the paddle into the container and produces a sample of fifty beads. This is repeated for several rounds, usually four or five, to simulate a number of workdays; willing workers produce one sample per day. After the willing workers produce their samples, they report to an inspector who counts defects. A defect is a red bead or a vacant indentation. The willing workers then report to a second inspector who makes a second count of defects. After making their counts, the inspectors report to the chief inspector who checks the results of the inspectors.

If the results are the same, the chief inspector reports the number to the recorder. If the results are not the same, the chief inspector counts the defects, reports that number to the recorder, and directs the willing worker to dump the beads back in the container and return to the work line. The recorder writes all results on a matrix that shows willing worker performance by day.

In practice, the facilitator of the experiment adds other, potentially confounding elements to the experiment. Willing workers are provided brief training and told they will have an apprenticeship period. They are then put directly to work without any period of apprenticeship. New workers who are added to the line as a result of dismissals are given no training. The facilitator announces a quota of no more than one red bead per day. The facilitator praises good performance, a very low number of defects, and condemns or punishes with dismissal poor performance, a very high number of defects. The facilitator may throw in quality slogans and generally exhort the willing workers to perform better. After several days of work, the facilitator threatens workers with dismissal because of their inconsistent and generally poor performance. After all, no one is meeting the quota of no more than one defect per paddle. The facilitator ensures that senior managers among the participant group are included in the willing worker group and, as the experiment progresses, points out their poor performance to the great glee of the other participants. Finally, when all workdays are complete, the facilitator closes the operation and tells all willing workers to collect their severance pay on the way out.

The matrix prepared by the recorder might look something like Figure 12.1.

Name	Mon	Tues	Wed	Thurs	Fri	Total	Average
Worker 1	17	6	7	6	5	41	
Worker 2	8	7	10	8	11	44	
Worker 3	9	9	14	16	12	60	
Worker 4	10	16	8	11	9	54	
Worker 5	10	10	10	7	8	45	
Worker 6	7	20	11	11	13	62	
Total	61	68	60	59	58	306	
Average							10.2

Figure 12.1.   Results of a red bead experiment.

The red bead experiment reveals much about system performance. While many system elements interact, in this case, materials determine results. The bead mixture is 80 percent white beads and 20 percent red beads. The paddle holds fifty beads. Given a fair product on effort by the worker—that is, the worker does not try to change results by quickly dipping the paddle again if it looks like a large number of red beads are on the paddle from the initial dip, or the worker does not bump the paddle against the container and knock some beads off—the number of red beads in each sample of fifty will be about 20 percent, or about ten. As expected, results in Figure 12.1 show an average of 10.2 red beads. As the number of samples increases, the average will get closer and closer to ten. Other factors may seem to influence results, but they are not relevant:

- **Inspections** (excessive) have no effect on system performance.
- **Quotas** have no effect on system performance.
- **Slogans** have no effect on system performance.
- **Exhortations** to do well have no effect on system performance.
- **Rewards and punishments** have no effect on system performance.
- **Management** (by the facilitator) has no effect on system performance.

In this case, the only thing that matters—the only factor that affects and determines system performance—is the percentage of red beads in the bead mix. The lesson is: Fix the system, do not blame the workers. It calls back to the 85/15 rule that says about 85 percent of a worker's performance is determined by the system and 15 percent is determined by individual effort. The bead mixture principally determines results. A worker can still influence results to a degree through careless performance (knocking beads from the paddle during production) or by cheating (dipping the paddle twice), but performance results are mostly a matter of materials, an aspect of the system that is beyond the worker's control.

The red bead experiment also reveals something about variation. The data in Figure 12.1 show an average number of defects of 10.2 per production, but individual production numbers vary from 5 to 20 defects. Each production of fifty beads will not be exactly the same; results will vary. How much they may be expected to vary can be determined by using a control chart and calculating upper and lower control limits. For these data, the upper and lower control limits are nineteen and two, respectively. Normal system performance will yield two to nineteen defects in any individual production. Workers should not be criticized or specially rewarded for performance within this range. Quotas should not be established outside this range. Slogans and exhortations should not address any performance outside this range.

What about worker 6 who produced twenty defects on Tuesday? How should management respond? Punish the worker? Recall that control limits do not encompass 100 percent of the data. Control limits are sometimes established at 3σ above and below the mean, which encompasses 99.73 percent of the data. The performance of twenty defects could be normal system performance that falls within the other 0.23 percent, or, if these data relate to performance that occurred after the control limits were established, the twenty defects could be a result of special cause variation acting on the system. Perhaps worker 6 was a new hire that joined the work line after the initial workers completed training and, therefore, received no training. An untrained worker is a source of special cause variation.

Using a control chart to analyze the data obtained during the red bead experiment shows that the system is stable and is producing predictable results. The red bead experiment is often an eye-opening experience for participants. It shows more clearly than any text can describe how systems influence results.

Practical Exercise

The following exercise allows readers to apply the concepts and tools presented in this book. Readers should complete the exercise, not simply scan the description and assume they "got it." Completing the exercise will solidify understanding of quality concepts and tools before readers attempt to apply them in real project practice.

Background

Beads R Us is a producer of high-quality plastic beads for commercial use. The production process is as described in the red bead experiment. Workers produce beads in lots of fifty by dipping a paddle into a bin of beads and withdrawing fifty at a time. Some of the beads are red; red beads are defective. If the production lot is less than fifty, the absent beads count as defects. Recently, management has become dissatisfied with the number of defects during production.

Beads R Us obtains materials from Bead World, one of three suppliers worldwide. Materials include defective beads, which must be eliminated prior to delivery to customers.

A major customer of Beads R Us has informed management that it will reject any future delivery that includes more than fifteen defective beads in a sample of fifty to be taken on the receiving dock at the time of delivery. Beads R Us has engaged your project team on a consulting contract to analyze its process, and identify any shortcomings, and recommend solutions.

Data Collection

Six members of your project team were secretly sent to Beads R Us as new employees to gain first-hand experience with the bead production process. They worked for five days before being withdrawn. The performance data for the six team members are summarized as shown in Figure 12.1.

The six team members also prepared a report of their work experiences. The key points in their report are summarized below.

1. Training is not good. New hires are not given any training. They are immediately placed on the production line and told to do what the person next to them is doing. Beads R Us calls this "on-the-job training."
2. Communication is not good. Workers are not allowed to ask questions and are not allowed to talk to each other while on the line. Anyone caught talking is punished. Beads R Us managers tell workers that there is no time for frivolous behavior. They are paid to work, not talk.
3. Management is not good. When things go well, managers take all the credit. When things do not go well, managers blame the workers and threaten punishment.

4. Leadership is not good. Managers are seldom seen on the production line. When they do show up, they walk quickly through the area and tell people to do better or their jobs are at risk.

5. The work environment is not good. The production area is covered with posters containing quality slogans such as "Mistakes cost us money," "Work hard, keep your job," "We're counting on YOU," and "No defect is a good defect." Workers have trouble understanding the meaning of these slogans and have no idea about how to implement them.

6. Quotas are unreasonable. Management has assigned quotas for production that have never been achieved by anyone. Managers continually harp on the quotas and threaten punishment of those who do not make quota.

7. Rewards are inconsistent and inequitable. Two people can produce the same quality and one gets a reward while the other does not. A worker can be rewarded one day for good performance and punished the next day for poor performance. A worker who performed particularly well one day received an on-the-spot bonus and a pin that said "Employee of the Day." The next day, the same employee was fired for poor performance.

Requirement

Apply your quality knowledge and meet all contractual requirements. Specifically:

- **Analyze** the process of bead production at Beads R Us.
- **Identify** any shortcomings that indicate inability to meet customer requirements.
- **Recommend** solutions that eliminate any shortcomings.

Tips

This practical exercise does not include a prescribed solution. Readers should be creative in their solution approach; results will vary from reader to reader. Readers should apply as many of the quality tools as possible. Some tools are intended for group use. Not all may be beneficial. Readers will better understand the utility and limitations of the tools as they try to put them to use. Here are some suggestions.

1. Collecting data
   - A **check sheet** might be prepared to show defects by day or by worker. The matrix in Figure 12.1 is already a collection of data.
2. Understanding data
   - A **line graph** or a **bar graph** might be used to show the progression of defects by worker over time. A **pie graph** might be used to show the number of defects by worker or by day relative to the total number of defects.
   - A **histogram** might be used to show how defects are distributed by worker or by day.
   - A **Pareto chart** might be used to identify defects in descending order by worker or by day of the week.
   - A **scatter diagram** might be used to investigate a possible relationship between days of the week and the number of defects produced.
3. Understanding processes
   - A **flow chart** might be used to better understand the steps in the bead production process.
   - A **run chart** might be used to understand how production progresses over time.
   - A **control chart** might be used to determine system performance and if expected performance meets customer requirements. (Hint: All 30 productions must appear on the x-axis, with the number of defects on the y-axis. They may be plotted either by worker/ by day or by day/by worker.)
4. Analyzing processes
   - A **cause and effect** diagram might be used to identify causes and root causes of defective beads. (Hint: When determining categories, consider the information provided by the six team members in their report.)
   - A **pillar diagram** might be used to identify the relationships between suspected causes and results.
5. Solving problems
   - **Force field analysis** might be used to identify and understand the forces that affect quality performance. It might provide a foundation for improvement action.
   - **Brainstorming** might be used to identify causes when using process analysis tools or to identify possible improvement actions.

- ◆ An **affinity diagram** might be used to organize and better understand the random results of brainstorming.
- ◆ **Nominal group technique** might be used to gain consensus on priorities of action to be recommended.

Recommendations should be presented to Beads R Us as a final report, with relevant quality tools attached for clarification and justification.

Summary

- ◆ When managing project quality, project managers must gain an appreciation for systems. They must understand the elements that work together to produce project results.
- ◆ Quality tools enable understanding of systems. They enable fact-based analysis and decisions that ensure delivery of quality products and services.

Points to Ponder

1. What is the basic message of the Red Bead Experiment? Why is this important in managing quality?
2. Discuss the practical or perhaps superficial utility of the various contributing factors by management in the Red Bead Experiment described in this chapter. Explain why these contributing factors may be in common use.

13

Why *Not* Quality?

In quality, it's what you *do* that counts—action. Quality does not arise from passive optimism. Quality does not appear because people hope things will get better. Recall the earlier statement that quality is counterentropic. Quality is not a naturally occurring event. Quality occurs only because someone makes it happen.

Making quality happen is not easy. Project managers and teams can have the best of intentions. They can have the necessary skills and tools. They can have at their disposal a proven model for quality management in a project context. And they can still run into a brick wall.

Quality Disablers

Quality is not only counterentropic, it can be the enemy of the natural order of things. Many factors of the natural order—common practice, if you will—can conspire to keep quality on the outside looking in. Here are some of them.

The Bottom Line

Whether in the ever-present pressure to increase revenue in a commercial setting, or the necessity to operate within existing budgets in a not-for-profit setting, or the desire to obligate current funds and thereby justify future funds at equivalent or higher levels in a government setting, the demands of the bottom line are always there. Quality may be a great concept, but it does not compete well with the realities of financial reports.

A technical services company was holding an annual conference call with its employees working in off-site locations distributed around the country. Senior executives provided updates on company performance and expectations for the future. All of this was couched in financial terms about current revenue and future goals. At the end of the presentations, employees were given an opportunity to ask questions. Some questions related to the financial information, but most related to company product quality and customer satisfaction. The employees were the ones who met the customers face-to-face and their questions reflected the concerns that arose from those encounters.

One bold employee commented about the inability to correct minor defects in company products, especially those identified by customers. He commented that "sometimes it seems we put cost over quality." The CEO responded. He assured the group that that would never happen. Product quality was a paramount concern and a hallmark of company performance. Then he added a dose of reality: "But I must warn you, quality does have a cost. We could put so much quality in our products that our customers could not afford them." This view, held by the most senior executive and woven throughout the fabric of the company, was the reason why minor defects went uncorrected. The fixes cost money and those costs cut into profits. A more effective response—for the long- and short-term—would have been, "We can put so much quality in our products that our customers cannot afford *not* to have them."

Reluctance to Change

Quality improvements involve change—doing something different. Change can be a risky and scary thing. People are reluctant to do risky and scary things. They would rather remain in their comfort zone of known things, regardless of the current condition, rather than step into the unknown.

This is nothing new. William Shakespeare addressed this in his play, *The Tragedy of Hamlet, Prince of Denmark*, written around 1600. In the play, Hamlet, the melancholy Dane, is deeply troubled. In his famous "To be, or not to be" soliloquy, he contemplates suicide as a means of ending his internal strife. But he defers out of fear of the future. His present situation may be bad, but his future situation could be a lot worse. Equating death with sleep, he says, "For in that sleep of death, what dreams may come…must give us pause." Modern clinical psychologists may confirm that the same view is alive and well today. It is not uncommon for a psychologist to work with a patient and over time, assess the situation, agree on the problem, and agree on a solution that will improve the situation only to have the patient reject the solution. The patient agrees with the problem and the solution, but is afraid that the solution, which involves a change and a step into the unknown, may result in a situation that is worse than the present. No matter how bad things are now, at least they are known.

In a project environment, this basic characteristic of human behavior can appear in the quality improvement option of, "Why don't we do nothing? Maybe it will get better by itself."

Offense at Improvement Suggestions

A project may seem to be a professional environment, but just below the surface things can be very personal. It may be difficult to agree as a group that it's okay to improve. A suggestion of an improvement opportunity may be viewed as criticism of those responsible for the current conditions, usually the boss. The suggestion then becomes viewed as disloyalty or even an act of aggression. Consider this brief conversation between the task manager (TM) and the project manager (PM).

TM: Bob? Gotta minute? I'd like to run something by you.

PM: Sure, but be brief. I'm a little busy.

TM: Okay, I'll cut to the chase. I've got an idea for quality improvement. On the Kelsey contract, we've been having some problems with our deliveries. Getting a lot of returns. So I took a look at...

PM: Wait a minute, wait a minute. Are you saying I'm doing a bad job?

TM: No, not at all, Bob. I just see a chance...

PM: Look, I'm in charge here. If things aren't going well, I'm going to get the blame.

TM: Bob, this isn't personal. We've got a team effort here and I think...

PM: Look, if you think that I'm going to tell my boss that the team I supervise isn't performing and I need to make some "quality" changes, you're crazy.

TM: Okay, never mind.

Wounded pride and hurt feelings are milder responses of this kind. They can have an adverse effect on working relationships within a team and, at worst, lead to reduced communication or desires to get even.

The common thread among situations like this is that quality improvement is a professional matter. Suggestions for improvement should be welcomed, not shunned. Significantly successful suggesters should be celebrated as heroes, not condemned as traitors. Each quality improvement provides a better view, which makes more opportunities visible and more improvement possible. Improvements can and should be continuous. The project will be better for it.

Problem-Solving versus Opportunity-Seeking

Project teams can develop an exclusive focus on problems—fixing things that will do harm—rather than looking for opportunities to do things better. This can be a limiting factor on overall project performance. The old adage, "If it ain't broke, don't fix it" says it best—or maybe worst. There is probably a kernel of wisdom in the adage: don't tinker around with things that work well. But applied more universally, usually unintentionally, this adage can put a severe damper on project performance. Even if something "ain't broke," it might be made better. And the opportunity to make something better might be hindered by the reluctance to tinker with something that is working well. Working well does not mean working best any more than "adequate" means "superior."

Project teams must actively seek opportunities. That's work...and maybe it is essential project work. There is another old adage: "Opportunity knocks but once." Again, there is probably a kernel of wisdom in this. But in the project world, opportunity does not knock, it taps very gently. Sometimes it just stands there silently waiting for you to open the door and discover its presence.

Dr. Deming made much of seeking opportunity for improvement in his book *Out of the Crisis*. Admonishing senior managers to get out on the floor and get directly involved in quality, he observed about a consulting stint in which he identified several improvement opportunities, that none of them would have happened if he had not been out looking for them.

Culture

The prevailing culture in an organization can have over-arching influence on all things the organization does. Organizations that focus outward on customers and markets are more likely to embrace quality than organizations that focus inwards on management and structures.

The culture that individuals carry with them is also important. Consider the individuals whose work culture is characterized by a top-down pyramid of *my customers, my products,* and *my capabilities.* Their capabilities—their knowledge, skill, and abilities—are the foundation for the new and innovative products that they develop and deliver to customers with whom they feel a personal connection. Such people are the bedrock of quality organizations. Now consider the individuals whose work culture is characterized by a top-down pyramid of *my salary, my job,* and *my subordinates.* Their subordinates—ever-increasing numbers of people controlled—are the foundation for enhanced and inflated job descriptions that support higher levels of salary, perquisites, and benefits. Such people are the bedrock of bureaucratic organizations in which quality cannot abide.

The Solution

Taken individually or collectively, the quality disablers described here can cast a pall of doom and gloom over a project team. The way out from under this is simple: what a psychologist might call the "will to quality," or perhaps more grammatically stated, the "will to improve." Just as a sports team must have the "will to win"—an inextinguishable desire to take the field, mix it up with the opposing team, and prevail utterly—a project team must have the will to do only quality work now and forever. No excuses, no whining, no sidestepping for whatever seems convenient at the moment. Only quality, and quality, and quality. Fundamentally, this will is not a group attribute. At its roots, it resides in individuals; it begins with people who can and must make a difference.

In quality, it's what *you* do that counts.

Summary

- Excessive focus on financial matters can hinder quality performance.
- Individual and organizational reluctance to change can hinder quality performance.
- Taking personal offense at suggestions for improvement can hinder quality performance.

- Focusing on solving problems to the exclusion of seeking improvement opportunities can hinder quality performance.
- Organization and individual culture that focuses internally can hinder quality performance.
- Hindrances to quality can be overcome by a simple and sincere will to improve by people in a quality organization.

Points to Ponder

1. How can excessive focus on the bottom line hinder quality in a project? What kind of financial goals or concerns can come into play?
2. Describe how reluctance to change can hinder quality in a project. Where does this reluctance come from?
3. How can taking offense at improvement suggestions hinder quality in a project? Why does this response occur?
4. Describe how excessive focus on solving problems can hinder quality in a project. Why might a project team focus on problems to the exclusion of other matters?
5. Explain how organization or individual culture can hinder quality in a project. Where does culture, both organizational and individual, come from? Can culture be changed?
6. Describe how the various disablers of quality may be overcome. Consider all of the disablers mentioned in this chapter.

Exercise

a. Do a mini-intervention in a project or work group to which you have access. Interview the members and explore the possible existence of the quality disablers described here.
b. If you feel confident, suggest a means of overcoming any of the disablers found to be present.
c. Present your results in class or to a collaborative work group.

This book has free material available for download from the
Web Added Value™ resource center at *www.jrosspub.com*

Epilogue

Dr. Deming would often close his lectures by saying, "Your life is forever changed. Tomorrow is a new day. Nothing will ever be the same." A cynic might think such pronouncements rather arrogant, but Dr. Deming was right. Having experienced the red bead experiment and understood its implications, no participant could go back to the old ways of thinking about quality. And *thinking* about quality is the first step toward *doing something* about quality.

Quality does not arise from whipping the oarsmen harder. It does not arise from scientific, detailed analysis to determine the one best method. There is no "one best method" and there are no standard, just-like-all-the-others workers. People are different. They come in different sizes and shapes. They possess and exhibit different motivations and attitudes. They have different skills and capabilities—and some days they are hot and some days they are not.

Quality is not a thing. Outside the natural world, there are no *things*. There are only things that *people* make or things that *people* do. Quality arises from people, people who make or do the things that other people buy or use. The project manager's obligation is to achieve the highest level of quality in meeting project goals and satisfying customer requirements and expectations. That is not a matter of chance. It is only possible through a deliberate effort to manage quality from the inception of the project idea, through project planning and implementation, to the delivery of the product of the project to the customer.

This book has proposed a method for managing project quality. To some, it may not be complete. To others, it may not be relevant. But to all, it is an opportunity to turn away from chance, or tradition, or whatever else has not worked well in the past and try something different. Considering the importance of project outcomes, it is an opportunity not to be ignored.

Appendix 1.
Case Study:
Dakota
Wireless Network

Background

The State of Dakota seeks to increase the investment of new business in the state by providing the best wireless communications environment in the country. Dakota has vast land areas suitable for high-tech business, but its limited communications infrastructure inhibits development. State planners realize that high-tech businesses depend on virtual teams supported by robust communications capabilities. The state recently issued a request for proposal (RFP) for the Dakota Wireless Network (DWN) with the following performance-based specifications:

   a. Design, install, and maintain a digital communications network that will allow—
   (1) Cell phone services for all state residents and businesses from any habitable point within state borders.
   (2) Wireless Internet connections for all state residents and businesses from any habitable point within state borders with download speeds of at least 200 Mbps at all times.
   (3) 99.99966 percent system availability at all times.
   b. Design and install network in a manner that minimizes environmental impact and community intrusion.
   c. Plan, prepare, conduct, and analyze public comment sessions as required.

   d. Design and prepare promotional media items intended to attract new business development to Dakota because of the unique capabilities of the DWN.

   e. Develop a course of instruction on "Virtual Teams for Project Management" that may be adopted without modification by all state colleges and universities as a three-credit undergraduate course.

   f. Develop and present as required a four-day seminar for professionals on "Virtual Teams for Project Management" that awards three undergraduate credits recognized by the American Council on Education.

   g. Comply with all applicable federal and state regulations.

The Project

Your company, JCN Networks, was recently awarded a five-year contract for the Dakota Wireless Network based on a specific proposal that took no exceptions to the RFP.

You were notified Sunday night by e-mail from the CEO that you have been selected as project manager. Key members of your project team have also been selected. Two of the six participated on the proposal team. They will all meet with you Monday morning at 8:30 a.m. in the conference room at corporate headquarters in Sioux River Station.

Appendix 2.
Project Training

Training is an important matter related to project quality. Inadequately trained project teams cannot be expected to perform in the stellar ways organizations and clients expect. Project managers should keep in mind that training is a means to an end, not an end in itself. This fact is often ignored by typical training measures of effectiveness such as the number of people trained or the amount of money spent on training.

Before getting to training itself, consider the larger issue—the end for which training is one of the means. The "end" is a quality workforce: a collection of people with the right skills available in the right place at the right time. There are several means by which a project manager may achieve this overall goal.

Internal Assignment

This is the fastest and probably least expensive way of building a project team. It is widely used for internal projects; that is, those performed by internal resources for an internal need under a project charter. It is also fraught with difficulty.

The big benefit is that the people are generally immediately available. The big problem is that the pool of potential team members is limited to those who *are* available. Everyone wants the best possible employees on their team. The best possible employees are always in high demand and usually fully booked. They are often not available or available only on a part-time basis. Part-time participation can be helpful as it adds a high level of expertise when needed, but it can also be problematic as it disrupts communication and work relationships.

The employees in the available pool may not be those with exact-match skills. A project manager may have to make do with "close enough" for the time being and deal with skill enhancement later.

The employees in the available pool may be available for a reason. The good reason is that they have successfully completed work on a closing project and need a new work assignment to maintain employment. The not-so-good reason is that their performance on their current project is in some way deficient. Not bad enough for disciplinary action or formal termination, but bad enough that their current project manager wants to cut them loose and pass them along to another project.

New Hires

This is the slowest and most expensive way of building a project team. It takes a long time and a lot of work to develop job descriptions, place announcements, identify candidates, conduct interviews, and complete all the associated human resources paperwork. And once you make a hire, that's it; there is no easy way to turn back if you decide that you did not make the right decision.

There is a degree of uncertainty in new hires. In spite of detailed résumés and comprehensive, sequential interviews, employers are never really sure about what they are getting. For that reason, personal referral is the most frequently used method of identifying and obtaining new hires. It's a rule of thumb among job seekers that you will probably be hired by someone "who knows who."

Project managers must exercise a little caution in personal referrals. The result may be a good personality match and a confidence-based relationship, but the ability to do the job should be the primary consideration. Consider the company that just won a contract to perform work at a client location several hundred miles away from headquarters. They send an experienced manger from headquarters to be the site manager and to build a project team. The manager has been around a while and has many professional contacts, including several at the new location. He contacts them and hires them as first-tier managers. These new managers, in turn, contact people with whom they have worked and whom they trust and hire them as the core staff. All is well and the team is off to a good start. Over time, the work requirements grow and the technical expertise and skills required soon exceed the capabilities of the original hires. But now the manager is stuck. These people are personal friends. He lured them away from secure jobs to join his team. He cannot terminate their employment because they can't do the job. He must train them up to the performance level required.

Personal referral is a quick and popular method for building effective teams. But in the end, hiring decisions must be rational and unbiased, based on the needs of the project.

Contract Labor

This is a quick way of getting temporary access to highly specialized skills or more general skills that are needed on a short-term basis. These types of needs are better met through a contract for a specific period than by hiring a new employee who may have to be terminated when the need no longer exists.

It is also a good model for organizations whose ongoing work consists of intermittent, unpredictable, short-term efforts. The labor force required can be brought to bear when necessary and not used when not necessary, unlike full-time employees who draw resources whether they are working on project tasks or not.

Contract labor may allow a trial period for potential new hires. A project manager could bring a candidate on-board as a contractor, either individually or through a temporary employment agency, and subsequently offer them a full-time job if things work well.

Training

Training is the classic method of improving the knowledge, skills, and abilities of the existing workforce. Project managers should apply training with care. They should not adopt an attitude of, "We've got a problem, and let's throw some training at it." They should not select and require training based on a seductive course title or an attractive promotional brochure. When selecting and applying training, a project manager should ask and answer several key questions.

1. What are the tasks required to be performed?
2. What are the skills required to perform those tasks?
3. To what degree do those skills exist in the current workforce?
4. What training is required to bring the skills up to the needed level?

5. What is the best source of and method for that training? (Conduct the training)
6. What was the effect of the training on the skill level in the workforce?
7. To what degree has the new skill level improved performance of the required tasks?

These questions are not easy to answer. Taken as a group, they can be rather intimidating. Questions 6 and 7 are absolutely essential but almost never asked or answered. But they are all important. They are the foundation for training as a means of improving project performance, not just training for training's sake.

Several methods of training are available to project managers. There is no "one size fits all." They are all dependent upon the situation and the people involved.

On the Job Training. This is a quick way of bringing a new member of the project team up to speed. It is also dangerous. Training while you work can establish bad habits that are difficult to diagnose and correct later on. Training by watching someone else may be little more than learning that person's errors and repeating them.

Training by Internal Staff. A project manager could tap into experts on the project team to present short seminars or "brown-bag" lunches that address a specific, short topic. This may have a positive team-building effect in that experts on the team are sharing their expertise with others for the overall benefit of the organization. On the other hand, subject matter experts are not necessarily the best teachers. Or, if the training includes short performance exercises, critiques of those exercises by the expert may generate hard feelings or resentment.

Online Training. This is a good delivery method for training matters of knowledge acquisition and is usually not expensive. It is good for small numbers of students or even individuals in remote locations. Because the training can be accessed at any time, it is good in situations where students are expected to complete the training on their own time or on paid time after-hours. A good example of this type of training is a class to prepare for the PMP® Certification Exam. The task is simply a matter of acquiring new knowledge and feeding it back during the exam. Concepts are not complex and shared, personal experience by either an instructor or other students has no relevance. Additionally, most courses—online or distributed on CD-ROM—include sample questions that mimic what is likely to be encountered on the exam. Students can drill these questions repeatedly and practice in the same way they will have to perform during the exam, which is administered online.

Instructor-Led, Classroom Training. This is the most expensive training of all. It requires time by the students that takes them off project work and is usually high-priced because of the associated costs for the delivering organization. It is the right delivery method—even the best method—for matters of skill refinement or knowledge acquisition involving novel or complex concepts. For matters of skill refinement, students get hands-on experience. Novel or complex concepts may be explored under the guidance of an expert instructor who can answer questions and clarify any confusion. Working with others, sharing their experiences, and learning from them in a practical sense can be far more beneficial than the solitary experience of an online course. Project managers may be able to reduce overall costs by bringing an instructor to the work location rather than send a large number of students to a training site. Most training companies are willing to do on-site delivery and do so at a reduced price because the project-provided facilities avoid a cost for them. There is a danger for the project team in on-site delivery. Students will be tempted—perhaps required—to return to their desks during breaks or lunch to check in on project work. They may get involved and return to class late and miss part of the training that was paid for. Or they may get really involved in project work and be distracted from the training during class and miss a lot of what is being presented. All of these drawbacks are manageable. A good example of this type of training is a course on project quality management. Some material is straight knowledge acquisition and not very difficult. But applying quality tools is a matter of skill refinement. Students will be better served by the opportunity to apply the tools to classroom problems than by simply reading about the tools. They will be better off downstream when they go back to the office and apply the tools to real project requirements using the tools for *the second time*, not the first time after an introduction in class. Some material is a matter of knowledge acquisition of novel or complex concepts. The use of control charts is a good example. In both of these cases—quality tools and novel concepts—students benefit from the shared experiences of the instructor and their fellow classmates.

Project training costs are usually borne by the project organization. Clients are very reluctant to pay for training. First, they tend to believe that they selected the organization during the proposal process based on the skills the organization offered—skills that were deemed to be adequate for performance and better than those offered by competing organizations. Second, even if a need arises during contract performance that requires a skill not considered during proposal evaluation, clients view the benefits of training for that skill as lasting far beyond the life of the contract. It is therefore something that the project organization should pay for.

When tying training to the workforce, some project managers show a reluctance to train project team members. They agree that training is a way of improving the skills of the project team and ultimate project performance. They also believe that training will enhance an individual's ability to seek and obtain new employment elsewhere. They don't want to enable team members to jump ship, so they don't train. This is just silly. If employees are looking for other jobs, there is a bigger problem with the team than avoiding training will solve. In fact, the lack of essential training may be a source of underlying dissatisfaction that causes employees to look elsewhere. As stated earlier, training is important. If you don't train, you can't perform.

Appendix 3.
Project Leadership

Abraham Lincoln said, "The dogmas of the quiet past, are inadequate to the stormy present." He said that when faced with a new challenge, people must "think anew and act anew" and then they could overcome the challenge. So it is with project leadership. The classic dogmas of the quiet past are still there—Maslow's hierarchy of needs, Alderfer's more practical existence-relatedness-growth theory, the ubiquitous Myers-Briggs Type Indicator—and they are all still relevant to some degree. But they are fundamentally inadequate to the stormy present. Project work is different from day-to-day operations. It is a new challenge. To meet the challenge, project managers must think anew and act anew. They must become project leaders, too.

The *PMBOK® Guide* defines a project as "a temporary endeavor undertaken to create a unique product, service, or result." This definition suggests explicitly and implicitly several aspects of projects that set them apart from day-to-day operations and typically associated leadership practice.

Temporary Organizations

Projects performed by temporary organizations are a settled fact of life in commercial business domains. When a project is initiated, a team comes together, performs the work, and upon completion goes apart. This can be a very unsettling condition for team members who are essentially working toward the end of their own jobs. While day-to-day operations workers can look forward to a bright future of continued employment and perhaps promotion and growth, project workers must look forward to a rather bleak future of inevitable work end and possible employment termination. Project workers must adopt a new mind-set, a new feeling of self-confidence and self-reliance, to survive and perhaps even thrive in project work.

Temporary organizations affect relationships among team members. The team members don't work together long enough or close enough to develop relationships of trust and mutual support. Some don't even bother to try because others won't be around long enough to matter. Yet, relationships are critical to building teams that will overcome adversity and accomplish tasks in spite of roadblocks encountered.

When Dr. Deming was conducting a seminar at a major defense educational institution, he opened his presentation by asking, "What should we talk about today?" One participant called out, "TQM!" and Dr. Deming replied, "What's that?" Another participant called out "Annual appraisals!" probably because annual appraisals are the subject of one of Deming's Deadly Diseases. Dr. Deming asked, "Why do we do annual appraisals?" A four-star general in attendance offered an answer: "So we can promote people." Dr. Deming thundered, "Oh come on now. Let's be serious." The general probably thought he *was* being serious. And he wasn't accustomed to being thundered at. He left at the first break and did not return. Dr. Deming went on to explain that promotion of employees is too important to be left to periodic cursory reviews of personnel records and subsequent votes by committees. Promotion should be accomplished only after years of personal association with the people involved. That may be very true and very ideal, but project teams do not have the luxury of time in matters of promotion or anything else related to the project work. They won't be around long enough.

Temporary organizations can have a slightly more sinister effect on relationships. While individual team members may be looking at possible termination at the end of the project, more savvy members realize that salvation lies in assignment to a new project at or just before the close of the current project. They understand that the key to that is not among their peers but among the senior managers who make those new assignments. So they cozy up to the senior managers and build bridges that will ensure when the axe falls at the end of the project, it falls on someone else. This very practical approach has a deleterious effect on relationships and teamwork among the project team.

Ad Hoc Organizations

Project organizations are assembled from available resources or built from new resources specific to the needs of the project. They lack the existing hierarchies and structures of functional organizations associated with day-to-day operations. They are more "play-as-you-go" in nature.

One of the little secrets of project organizations is that there can be an underlying sameness among them that is a result of the common pool from which they all draw their resources. In any given geographical region, there is a relatively well-defined and somewhat fixed pool of labor. If a contract ends but is followed by a re-competition for continuing work, the winning bidder of the re-competition, if it is not the originally performing organization, may simply hire most of the staff of the old project team and put them to work on the new contract.

This revolving-door situation can lead to some shady dealings. A technical services company had an engineering-and-integration contract with a large government organization in which they provided Ph.D.-level expertise to assist the government in evaluating the performance of the more hands-on contractors. One of their project managers reviewed some reports of work performed by a hands-on contractor and found the work wanting. He wrote a critical evaluation. A few days later, he was visited by a project manager from the contractor whose work he had reviewed. The visitor thanked the reviewing project manager for the honesty and completeness of his review and said it would be helpful for making improvements and doing better in the future. Then he reminded the project manager that they were "all in this together." The way things go, you never know what the relationships might be in the future. One year I might work for you and the next year you might work for me. He suggested that the project manager recall his critical evaluation and give the hands-on organization a pass. This would be a good step in building long-term relationships. The reviewing project manager smiled politely and honorably showed him the door.

Eclectic Mixtures of Staff

Project organizations can have a broader mix of skills than the functional organizations associated with day-to-day work, with fewer individuals for each skill. Functional organizations exhibit a great commonality of skills. That's why they are called "functional." A functional organization might have 20 or 30 people who all do the same thing. A project organization might have two or three, or maybe just one. This puts a great burden of independence on the members of the project team. There may be no one to bounce things off of, no backup, no mentoring, and no one to commiserate with when things go bad.

Consider Molly, a violist with a large symphony orchestra. She is one of five or six musicians in the viola section. They all play the same music. There is a Principal Chair who may give some general guidance or specific directions on bowing for a particularly tricky passage, but generally they all do the same thing, together. When they get to the short dance-like section in Richard Strauss's *Till Eulenspiegel's Merry Pranks*, it's all violas. And the performance rises or falls based on their ability to play together.

Now consider Molly, the violist in a top-notch string quartet. There are no other viola players. She is all alone. No backup, no mentoring, no commiserating. When they play the opening bars of Smetana's *String Quartet No. 1 in E minor*, it's all Molly. And the performance rises or falls based on her ability to play the part perfectly, integrated conversationally with the perfect playing of the other three members of the quartet.

Project organizations are similar. They are characterized by a broad range of skills with a small number of team members for each skill. In some cases the skills can be so numerous and different and the individual experts so few that the project is more a loose confederation of independent experts than an integrated multifunctional team.

Unique Ends

Project results are, by definition, unique. Day-to-day operations churn out similar results again and again. Project results are one-of-a-kind, even when they may be similar. A construction company builds bridges, maybe many bridges. A casual view may suggest similar results, but in fact, no single bridge is built using exactly the same design, in exactly the same way, under exactly the same conditions. Each bridge is unique.

For the project team, this means that every project is a new experience. Every project includes doors that will open and disclose new surprises. This can be an uncomfortable experience for team members who yearn for routine or the familiarity of repeated experience.

These aspects of project work have significant implications for project leadership. As with leadership in general—and quality in general for that matter—there is no instant pudding; no off-the-shelf common approach to leadership that may be effectively applied in all settings. Project managers must be aware of these aspects. Recall that project management is the "accidental profession" that pulls outstanding performers from functional areas and makes them project managers. Project managers must go into project environments aware of the aspects described earlier and prepared to lead in a way that will respond to the conditions and avoid or mitigate any of the potential negative effects.

No recipe for project leadership will be proposed here. There exists an extensive body of literature that offers myriad recipes for different situations and tastes. Instead, project managers are urged to recognize that in project work, the executive role includes both management and leadership. The difference between the two has been well-studied and is well-represented in the literature. Management and leadership have been compared and contrasted over time by many experts. The link has been succinctly stated by several:

◆ Management is coping with complexity. Leadership is coping with change. (John P. Kotter)
◆ Managers are people who do things right and leaders are people who do the right things. (Warren Bennis)
◆ Leadership is applied to people, management is applied to things.

The last statement is a synthesis of general concepts expressed in the literature. More so than the others, it gets to the heart of the matter faced by project managers. A project manager must deal with people *and* things. Traditionally, the emphasis has been on the latter. Confirming this, John P. Kotter has famously said that American business is overmanaged and underled. The *PMBOK® Guide* and most project management literature focuses on the triple constraint of time, cost, and scope. These elements deal with things, but they are all things that do not exist without people. Time is an expression of how long it takes people to do something. Cost is an expression of the amount of resources people expend in doing something. Scope is an expression of what people do.

People and things are different. The tools and techniques applied when dealing with them are different. Management is about things and attributes. It's about *controlling* them in an effective and efficient way. Leadership is about people and behavior. It's about *releasing* the full power of people's knowledge, skills, and abilities and gaining people's best effort to do a job that they believe is important. In one sentence:

Management is holding on, leadership is letting go.

And that's a problem for project managers. As managers, they must control the raging elements of project performance that, like wild horses, could in a moment run amok and bring the project to a disastrous end. Then they run smack into the requirement of letting go as leaders—of releasing the controls and restraints that limit people in their quest to do their best, in their quest for project excellence. This is an inherent conflict in project management. Project managers must recognize it and resolve it effectively.

Abraham Lincoln said, "The occasion is piled high with difficulty, and we must rise—with the occasion." Different aspects, people, and things can conspire in a congress of complexity to confound the best-intentioned and most able project manager. Projects can be piled high with difficulty. Management is one track on the path to a successful end. Leadership is the other. Regardless of the tools used—the many and varied concepts, paradigms, and ways—project managers must rise with the occasion. They must do both.

Appendix 4.
Leading Change:
A Model by John Kotter

Change is a matter of central concern to project managers. In their book, *Project Manager's Portable Handbook*, David I. Cleland and Lewis R. Ireland state, "Projects are the principal means by which the organization deals with change." While projects may be the mechanism for change, the actual how-to steps of implementing change are often a frustrating, unsolved mystery.

John Kotter, the Konosuke Matsushita Professor of Leadership at the Harvard Business School, has developed a model for leading change that offers a valuable tool to project management professionals. His model is a result of many years of experience in consulting with hundreds of organizations. He observed the myriad difficulties associated with change efforts, distilled the common themes, and turned them around into a prescriptive framework.

But first, a little background. This difficulty with change is nothing new. In 513 B.C., Heraclitus of Greece observed, "There is nothing permanent except change." And in the 16th century, Niccolo Machiavelli stated in his political treatise, *The Prince*,

> *There is nothing more difficult to take in hand, more perilous to conduct, or more uncertain in its success, than to take the lead in the introduction of a new order of things.*

The challenge today is that change is not an "engineering" problem. Change involves people, and can call up emotions, uncertainties, and inconsistencies. Because of this, *managing* change is simply not sufficient. Leadership is necessary. The old saying, "You can lead a horse to water, but you can't make it drink" provides good advice, though slightly off the mark. It might be better stated, "You can manage a horse to water, but you must lead it to drink." Getting the horse to the water is a control issue that can be managed. Getting the horse to drink is a behavior issue that demands leadership.

When dealing with people and change, American social psychologist Kurt Lewin observed during the 1940s that a successful change includes three progressive steps:

♦ Unfreezing the present level of performance
♦ Moving to a new level
♦ Freezing group life at the new level

Lewin also stated, "To break open the shell of complacency and self-righteousness it is sometimes necessary to bring about deliberately an emotional stir-up."

Kotter's model suggests a similar three-part framework:

♦ Defrost the *status quo*.
♦ Take actions that bring about change
♦ Anchor the changes in the corporate culture.

The first element, "defrost the *status quo*," comprises four essential steps. First, leaders must establish a sense of urgency. People must have a reason, and a really good one at that, for doing something different. Leaders should examine market or competitive realities and identify an urgent need in terms of a crisis, potential crisis, or great opportunity. This is not a sky-is-falling scare tactic. It is a necessary step to jolt people out of complacency—to make them believe that the current situation is more dangerous than leaping into the unknown. This is a critical first step. In Kotter's experience, 50% of change efforts failed right here. His studies further suggest that about 75% of the work force must accept the "urgency" if the overall effort is to succeed.

The second step is to form a guiding coalition. Change cannot be directed through the existing hierarchy. It must be nurtured and supported by a dedicated group of influential leaders throughout the organization. The group may be small or large. It will probably not include the complete corporate leadership because of some reluctance to buy it. But it must be influential in order to lead the change. Without sufficient influence and power, the group will lead only *apparent* change. Over time, opposition forces will gain strength and snuff out the effort.

Third, leaders must create a vision. Once people accept the urgency, they want to know where they are going—they want a clear direction to a better future. Without a vision, the change effort can dissolve into a series of incompatible projects that start to look like change for change's sake. Failed change efforts are often littered with plans and directives, but no codifying vision. The vision must be clear and concise. It's not much good if it makes great copy, but nobody can understand it. Kotter suggests that leaders should be able to communicate the vision in five minutes and elicit understanding and interest. If not, they should rework the vision.

The fourth step, previewed just above, is to communicate the vision. The best vision in the world has no value if it's a big secret. Communication is more than a corporate announcement or a notice posted on the bulletin board. Leaders must communicate the vision through their actions. Sure, all the typical communication media play a part. But leaders must make opportunities to communicate the vision in day-to-day activities. For example, when presenting an award, a leader should take a moment to explain how the employee's performance fits into the vision and how the performance is a contribution to something much larger than the act being rewarded. More important, the day-to-day actions of leaders must reflect the vision. Nothing will kill a change effort quicker than leaders saying one thing and doing another.

Kotter cautions that a results-oriented leader may want to skip one or more of these first four steps in order to get right to the action. Doing so imperils, perhaps even condemns, the change effort. Without the solid foundation established by all of these steps, any change action is unlikely to take hold and survive for the long term.

The second element of the model includes three steps. This is the action element, and the first step is to empower others to act on the vision. Leaders must clear the way for employees to develop new ideas and approaches without being stymied by the old ways. The guiding coalition must remove obstacles that may be entrenched in organization processes, or exist only in the minds of employees. Both can be showstoppers. Kotter warns that worst of all can be the bosses who will not change and who make demands contrary to the vision. Such people should be given the opportunity to get on board and embrace the vision. Those who will not…well, a corporate turnaround expert once observed, "Sometimes you gotta change the people, or you gotta change the people."

The second action step is to plan for and create short-term wins. People will not follow a vision forever. Employees must see results within 12 to 24 months or they will give up or perhaps even join the naysayers. Short-term wins validate the effort and maintain the level of urgency. Leaders may have to look for things that disclose unambiguous benefits of the change effort. Rewarding people responsible for the benefits is essential.

The third step arises from the second: consolidate improvements and produce still more change. Short-term wins can be seductive. It can be easy to declare the battle won based on early benefits. Doing so can be fatal. Premature victory celebrations can quash momentum and allow the forces of tradition to regain their hold. Short-term wins must be stepping-stones to greater opportunities and bigger wins, all consistent with the vision driving the overall effort.

Kotter adds another word of caution that action alone is not enough. Any change, even that undertaken with great effort over an extended time, will wither unless it is reinforced within the organization. Leaders must not stop here; they must follow through with the next element.

The third and last element is a single step. Having made effective changes, leaders must now make the changes permanent. The forces of recidivism are still alive and well. Leaders must connect new behavior with corporate success, showing that the new ways are here to stay. Just as important, new leaders in the organization must espouse the new approaches. All that was accomplished can be undone by a change in leadership that bends back to the old ways.

Kotter's model for leading change is summarized below:

Lay the groundwork for change actions. Defrost the *status quo*

- Establish a sense of urgency
- Form a powerful guiding coalition
- Create a vision
- Communicate the vision

Take action for change

- Empower others to act on the vision
- Plan for and create short-term wins
- Consolidate improvements and produce still more change

Make the change permanent

◆ Institutionalize new approaches

Heraclitus, Machiavelli, and many others all had it right. Change is omnipresent, uncertain, and hard. But it is not impossible. Kotter's model for *leading change* provides a framework that may be applied in any organization at any level. It is a powerful tool for project managers or others who must lead their organizations into a better future.

This brief discussion is only an introduction to leading change. More information may be obtained from the sources listed below:

Kotter, John P. *Leading Change*. Harvard Business Review Press. Boston, MA. 2013.

Kotter, John P. and Cohen, Dan S. *The Heart of Change: Real-Life Stories of How People Change Their Organization*. Harvard Business Review Press. Boston, MA. 2013.

Kotter, John and Rathgeber, Holger. *Our Iceberg Is Melting*. St. Martin's Press. New York, NY. 2006.

Index